ORDNANCE MAINTENANCE

U.S. Rifles, Cal. .30, M1903, M1903A1, M1903A3 and M1903A4

WAR DEPARTMENT • *20 JANUARY 1944*

FOR ORDNANCE PERSONNEL ONLY

DISCLAIMER:

THIS MANUAL IS SOLD FOR HISTORIC RESEARCH PURPOSES ONLY, AS AN ENTERTAINMENT. IT CONTAINS OBSOLETE INFORMATION AND IS NOT INTENDED TO BE USED AS PART OF AN ACTUAL OPERATION OF MAINTENANCE TRAINING PROGRAM. NO BOOK CAN SUBSTITUTE FOR PROPER TRAINING BY AN AUTHORIZED INSTRUCTOR.

ORDNANCE MAINTENANCE

U.S. Rifles, Cal. .30, M1903, M1903A1, M1903A3 and M1903A4

WAR DEPARTMENT   •   *20 JANUARY 1944*

*This Technical Manual supersedes TM 9-1270, dated 19 May 1942; TB 1270-1, dated 1 May 1942. (It does not affect TB 1205-2, dated 1 May 1942); and TB 1270-2, dated 15 December 1942.

WAR DEPARTMENT

Washington 25, D. C., 20 January 1944

TM 9-1270, Ordnance Maintenance: U.S. Rifles, cal., 30, M1903,. M1903A1, M1903A3 and M1903A4, is published for the information and guidance of all concerned.

⎡ A.G. 300.7 (30 Aug 43) ⎤
⎣ O.O. 461/40925 O.O. ⎦

BY ORDER OF THE SECRETARY OF WAR:

G. C. MARSHALL,
Chief of Staff.

OFFICIAL:

J. A. ULIO,
Major General,
The Adjutant General.

DISTRIBUTION: R 9 (4); Bn 9 (2); C 9 (5).

(For explanation of symbols, see FM 21-6.)

CONTENTS

*This Technical Manual supersedes TM 9-1270, dated 19 May 1942; TB 1270-1, dated 1 May 1942; (it does not affect TB 1205-2, dated 1 May 1942); and TB 1270-2, dated 15 December 1942.

ORDNANCE MAINTENANCE — U.S. RIFLES, CAL. .30
M1903, M1903A1, M1903A3 AND M1903A4

Section I

INTRODUCTION

1. SCOPE.

a. This Technical Manual is published for the information and guidance of ordnance maintenance personnel. It contains detailed instructions for disassembly, assembly, inspection, maintenance, and repair of the materiel listed below. Additional descriptive matter and illustrations are included to aid in providing a complete working knowledge of the materiel. These instructions are supplementary to those in Field Manuals and Technical Manuals prepared for the using arms.

Rifle, U. S., cal. .30, M1903
Rifle, U. S., cal. .30, M1903A1
Rifle, U. S., cal. .30, M1903A3
Rifle, U. S., cal. .30, M1903A4 (Snipers)
Sight, telescopic, M73B1 (Weaver No. 330 C)
Bayonet, M1905
Bayonet, M1
Scabbard, bayonet, M3
Scabbard, bayonet, M1910
Scabbard, bayonet, M7
Sling, gun, M1907
Sling, gun, M1
Cover, front sight

b. This manual differs from TM 9-1270, Ordnance Maintenance: Rifles, U. S., cal, .30, M1903 and M1903A1, dated 19 May 1942 as follows:

(1) Information added on U. S. Rifles M1903A3 and M1903A4 (Snipers), Bayonet M1, Bayonet Scabbard M7, and Gun Sling M1.

(2) Information added on telescopic sight used with the Rifle M1903A4 (Snipers). This information is supplementary to that contained in TM 9-270.

(3) Changes in information contained in sections on maintenance and repair and special maintenance.

2. GENERAL.

a. The basic rifle of the group covered in this manual is the U. S.

INTRODUCTION

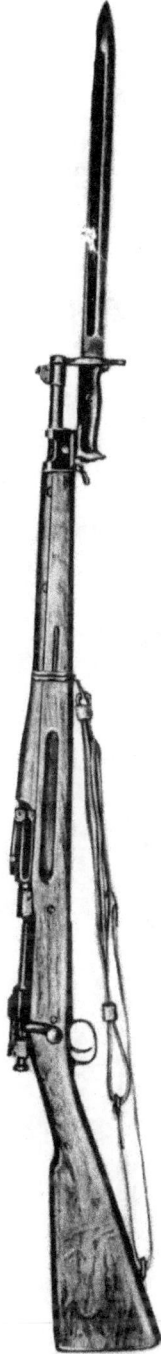

A. RIGHT SIDE VIEW   RA PD 7599

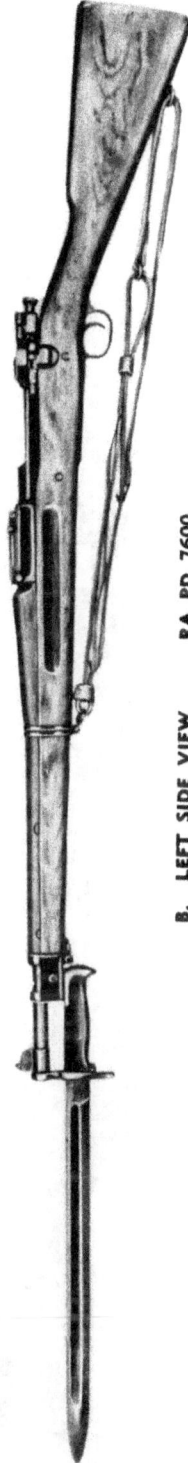

B. LEFT SIDE VIEW   RA PD 7600

Figure 1 — U.S. Rifle, cal. .30, M1903 With Bayonet M1905 and Sling M1907

ORDNANCE MAINTENANCE — U.S. RIFLES, CAL. .30,
M1903, M1903A1, M1903A3 AND M1903A4

A. RIGHT SIDE VIEW   RA PD 7601

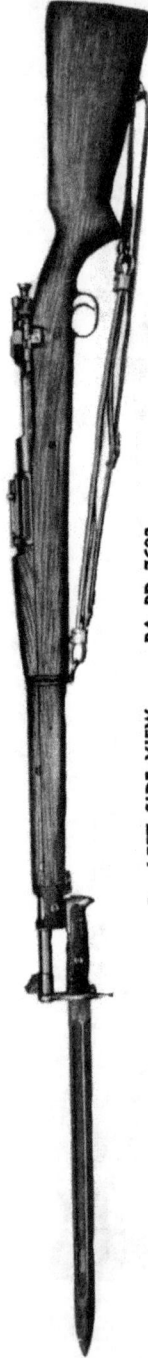

B. LEFT SIDE VIEW   RA PD 7602

Figure 2 — U.S. Rifle, cal. .30, M1903A1 With Bayonet M1905 and Sling M1907

INTRODUCTION

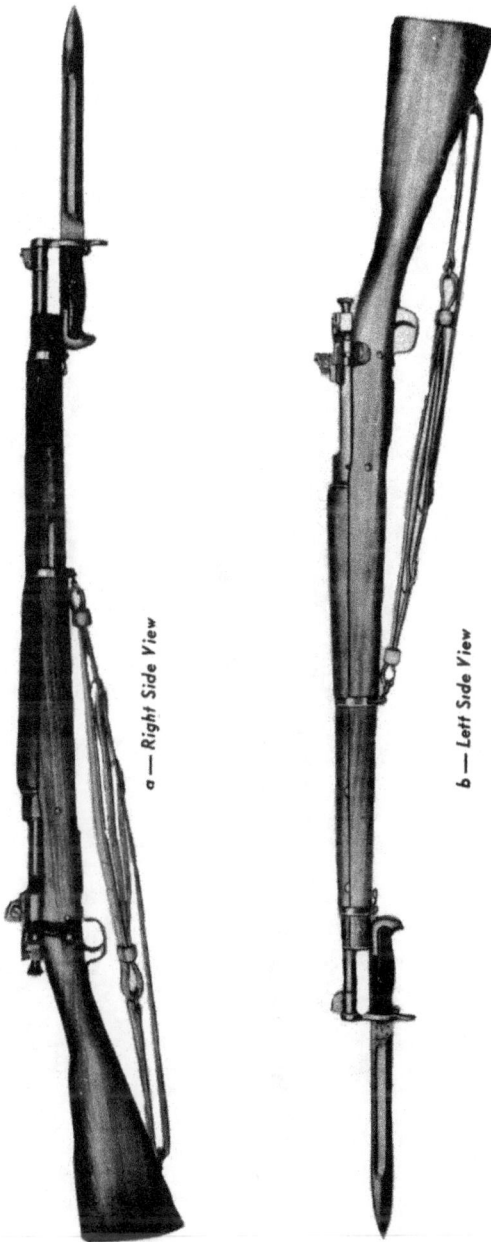

a — Right Side View

b — Left Side View

RA PD 79912

Figure 3 — U.S. Rifle, cal. .30, M1903A3 With Bayonet M1 and Sling M1907

ORDNANCE MAINTENANCE — U.S. RIFLES, CAL. .30,
M1903, M1903A1, M1903A3 AND M1903A4

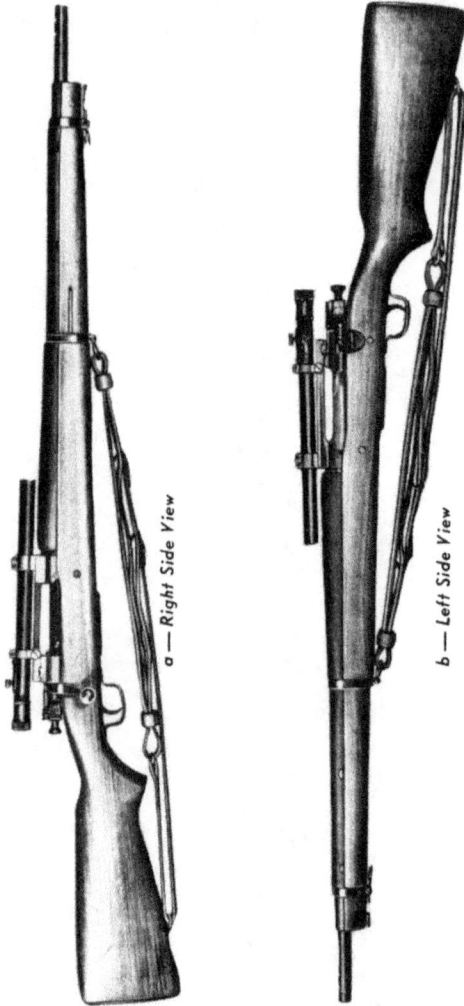

a — Right Side View

b — Left Side View

RA PD 79913

Figure 4 — U.S. Rifle, cal. .30, M1903A4 (Snipers) With Telescopic Sight M73B1
(Weaver No. 330 C) and Sling M1907

INTRODUCTION

Rifle, cal. .30, M1903 (fig. 1). This rifle, generally known as the Springfield rifle, has been in service for many years. Subsequently a pistol grip type stock replaced the straight grip type stock and, with the rifle so modified, the designation was changed to U. S. Rifle, cal. .30, M1903A1 (fig. 2). Later, the Rifle M1903 was modified in manufacturing details, the rear sight and fixed base removed and an adjustable rear sight of different design mounted on the bridge of the receiver, a barrel guard longer than and substituted for the hand guard, and a stacking swivel band added. This modified rifle was designated as U. S. Rifle, cal. .30, M1903A3 (fig. 3). Still later, the Rifle M1903A3 was modified by removing front and rear sight groups, assembling an M1903A1 type stock, mounting a telescopic sight on the top of the receiver, and designated as U. S. Rifle, cal. .30, M1903A4 (Snipers) (fig. 4). Detailed characteristics of the various models are explained in paragraph 3. An enlarged view of the mid-sections of the M1903A1, M1903A3, and M1903A4 Rifles is shown in figure 5 for the purpose of easy identification.

NOTE: Recently manufactured stocks do not have the grooves cut in the sides for gripping, as shown in figure 1.

b. As the Rifle M1903 is the basic rifle and the Rifle M1903A1 identical with the exception of the stock, these two may be considered as one rifle in this manual. As all of the four rifles covered herein are basically the same in mechanism, operation, and functioning, the disassembly and assembly, inspection, maintenance, and repair are covered to apply generally. Exceptions with regard to the models are noted where they apply. General illustrations are of the Rifle M1903A1, but apply to the other models unless specified otherwise in the text. Likewise, illustrations of the Rifle M1903A3 apply to the M1903A4 unless specified otherwise.

c. A list of parts for all four rifles covered herein is contained in SNL B-3, with parts common to any one model only, so indicated.

3. CHARACTERISTICS.

a. U. S. Rifle, Cal. .30, M1903.

(1) LOADING. This rifle is a breech-loading magazine weapon of the bolt type. The magazine will hold five cartridges, and one additional cartridge may be inserted in the chamber, thus making the maximum capacity for any one loading six shots. To facilitate the loading of the magazine, cartridges are ordinarily put up in brass clips holding five cartridges each. The magazine, however, may be loaded by inserting single cartridges by hand, one after the other.

(2) REAR SIGHT (fig. 6).

(a) The rear sight is adjustable for windage, and the drift of the bullet to the right is offset automatically by the construction of the rear sight leaf. The leaf is graduated from 100 to 2,850 yards. The lines extending completely across the branches of the leaf are alternate

ORDNANCE MAINTENANCE — U.S. RIFLES, CAL. .30,
M1903, M1903A1, M1903A3 AND M1903A4

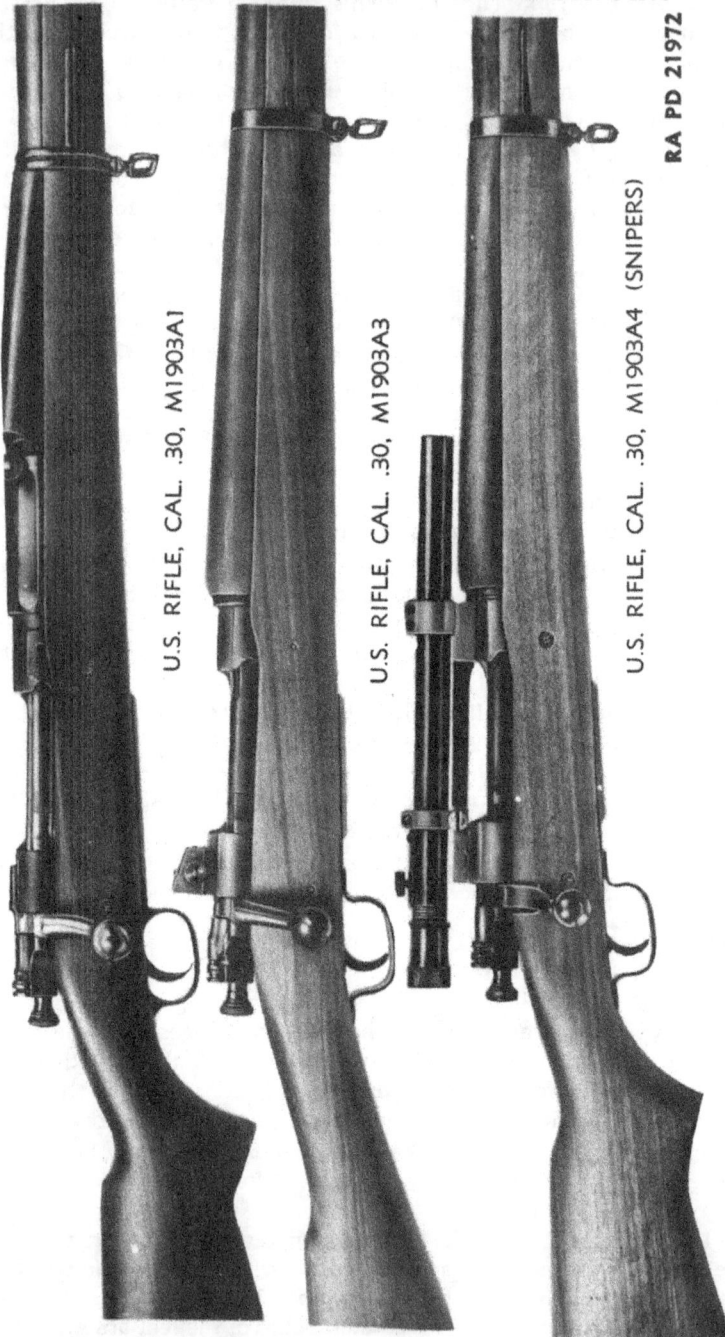

RA PD 21972

U.S. RIFLE, CAL. .30, M1903A1

U.S. RIFLE, CAL. .30, M1903A3

U.S. RIFLE, CAL. .30, M1903A4 (SNIPERS)

Figure 5—U.S. Rifles, cal. .30, M1903A1, M1903A3, and M1903A4 (Snipers)—Midsection—Right Side View
— Showing Characteristics for Identification

INTRODUCTION

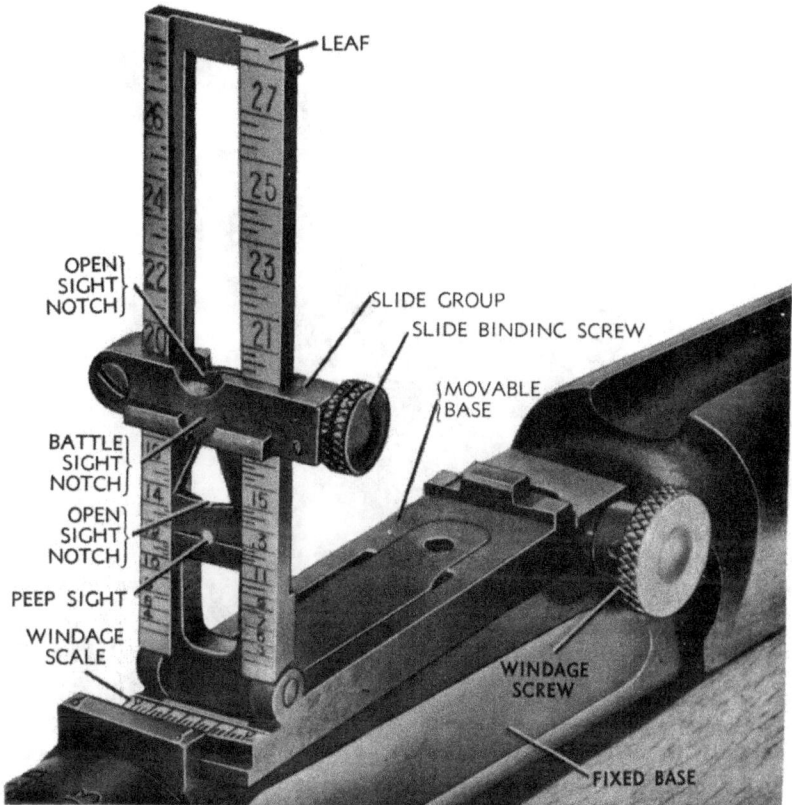

RA PD 84295

Figure 6 — Rear Sight Group Showing a Setting for Range and Windage — U.S. Rifles, cal. .30, M1903 and M1903A1

100-yard divisions, the longer of the short lines 50-yard, and the shorter lines 25-yard divisions. The drift slide, which may be moved up or down on the leaf, has two notches called open sights and a circular hole called the peep sight. With the leaf raised to the vertical position, the lines on either side of the peep sight and on either side of the lower open sight notch enable the user to set the drift slide accurately at any desired graduation on the leaf. With the leaf and slide in the down position, and using the battle sight notch which is cut in the slide cap, the sights are set for 547 yards.

(b) The rear end of the rear sight movable base is marked with wind gage graduations. Each graduation corresponds to a lateral deviation in the point of impact of the bullet of 4 inches for each 100 yards of range to the target.

(3) RATE OF FIRE AND EFFECTIVE RANGE. The maximum rate

ORDNANCE MAINTENANCE — U.S. RIFLES, CAL. .30,
M1903, M1903A1, M1903A3 AND M1903A4

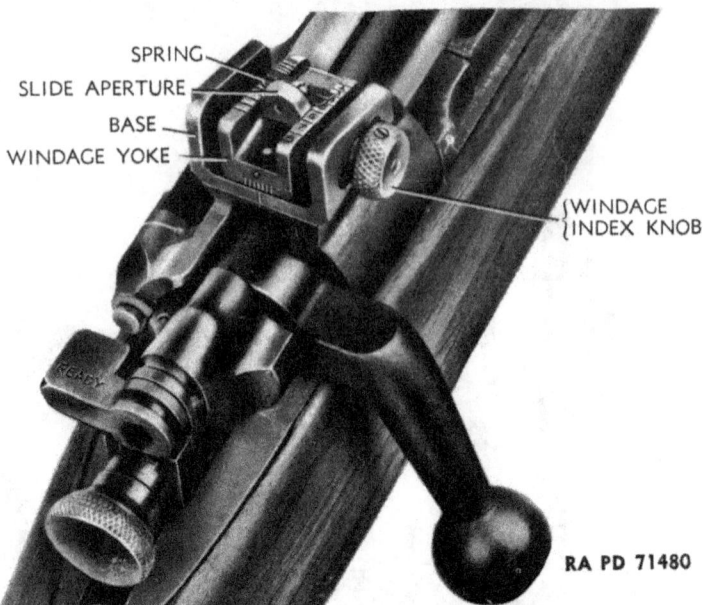

SPRING
SLIDE APERTURE
BASE
WINDAGE YOKE
{WINDAGE
{INDEX KNOB

RA PD 71480

Figure 7 — Rear Sight Group — U.S. Rifle, cal. .30, M1903A3

of accurate fire with this weapon depends upon the skill and the position of the operator and the visibility of the target. It varies from 10 to 15 shots per minute. The effectiveness of rifle fire during combat decreases as the range to the target increases. Its use at ranges greater than 600 yards is unusual.

(4) BORING. Originally the barrel of this rifle was bored with four grooves with a right-hand twist, and 1 turn in 10 inches. Recently manufactured barrels are bored similarly but with only two grooves instead of four. This change in boring applies to all models of this rifle covered in this manual.

b. **U. S. Rifle, Cal. .30, M1903A1.** This rifle is identical with the Rifle M1903 described in subparagraph a, above, with the exception of the stock assembly. The Rifle M1903A1 has a pistol grip type stock whereas the Rifle M1903 has a straight grip type stock.

c. **U. S. Rifle, Cal. .30, M1903A3.** This rifle is basically identical with the Rifle M1903 described in subparagraph a, above. Principal variations are in the front and rear sight groups and the design of a few parts as explained below. Like parts are not all interchangeable, and replacements should be made according to parts listed in SNL B-3.

NOTE: Parts of the Rifle M1903A3 which vary in design may be found in recently manufactured M1903 and M1903A1 Rifles, provided they are interchangeable.

INTRODUCTION

(1) STOCK. The stock is similar to that of the Rifle M1903, except that the pistol grip is optional on the M1903A3, whereas the M1903 did not have the pistol grip. Some of the M1903A3 Rifles issued had front and rear stock screw pins running laterally through the center portion of the stock to reinforce the trigger guard and magazine aperture in place of the front and rear stock screws and nuts assembled to the Rifle M1903. Front and rear stock screws and nuts are now standard for the Rifle M1903A3.

NOTE: SCREW, stock, front, B146876, is now used for both front and rear and nomenclature changed to "SCREW, stock."

(2) REAR SIGHT. In this rifle, the folding leaf type of rear sight and fixed base, such as used on the Rifles M1903 and M1903A1, are removed from the rear end of the barrel; and a rigid, wing type of rear sight is assembled to the bridge of the receiver (fig. 7). This sight consists of a base, windage yoke, slide aperture, spring, and windage index knob, and their components. The range scale on the windage yoke is marked in 100-yard graduations, and has 50-yard adjustments. The slide aperture can be moved up and down this scale for various ranges. Turning the windage index knob moves the yoke to the right or left to allow for windage. Each click represents a change of 1 minute of angle or a horizontal change of impact of 1 inch at a range of 100 yards. Each division or mark on the windage scale represents 4 minutes of angle or a change in the point of impact of 4 inches at a range of 100 yards.

(3) BARREL GUARD. In this rifle, a barrel guard (fig. 53) extending from the bayonet stud band to the front face of the receiver, takes the place of the hand guard (fig. 45) on the Rifle M1903 which extends from the upper band to the front face of the fixed base of the rear sight. (The bayonet stud band (fig. 53) corresponds to the upper band (fig. 51) of the Rifle M1903.)

(4) STACKING SWIVEL, BAYONET STUD BAND, AND LOWER BAND ASSEMBLIES (fig. 53).

(a) The stacking swivel is of stamped metal and secured to the forward end of the stock just to the rear of the bayonet stud band, by the stacking swivel band. In the Rifle M1903, the stacking swivel is of round wire and pivoted to the upper band.

(b) The bayonet stud band which replaces and is shorter than the upper band of the Rifle M1903, is solid on top and has two bayonet mounting studs on the bottom. In the Rifle M1903 there is an opening in the top of the upper band, and but one bayonet stud.

(c) The lower band swivel is a flat metal stamping pivoted in a flat lower band. The swivel in the Rifle M1903 is of round wire, and the lower band is grooved for reinforcement.

(5) TRIGGER GUARD MAGAZINE ASSEMBLY (fig. 49).

(a) The magazine, trigger guard, and floor plate are of stamped sheet metal, staked and welded together to form a single unit, and

ORDNANCE MAINTENANCE — U.S. RIFLES, CAL. .30,
M1903, M1903A1, M1903A3 AND M1903A4

called the "trigger guard magazine assembly." In the Rifle M1903, the magazine and trigger guard are an integral machined piece called the "trigger guard," and the floor plate is a separate machined piece assembled to the bottom of the magazine section of the trigger guard by means of a spring-operated catch assembled to the trigger guard (fig. 47).

(b) In the Rifle M1903, the magazine spring is clipped to the follower and floor plate, and the spring and follower are removed from the receiver together with the floor plate by disengaging the floor plate catch. In the Rifle M1903A3, the magazine spring is clipped to the follower only, which may be either the M1903 or M1903A3 follower, and must be removed from the top opening of the magazine, or together with the trigger guard magazine assembly as explained in paragraph 7 d.

(6) FRONT SIGHT GROUP (fig. 54). The front sight group is composed of a flat front sight pinned in a slot in a ring type sight base which is keyed and pinned to the muzzle end of the barrel. The sight is furnished in five heights, from 0.537 inch to 0.477 inch. The front sight group of the Rifle M1903 is composed of a flat front sight, a movable stud, and a fixed stud (fig. 51) which are assembled and pinned to each other and to a spline on the barrel.

(7) BUTT PLATE AND SWIVEL GROUP (fig. 50). This group is similar to that of the Rifle M1903 but composed of metal stampings instead of machined pieces. The butt plate trap is fastened in the butt plate assembly and not easily removable as in the case of the butt plate cap M1903 (fig. 48).

(8) BOLT GROUP (fig. 43). The parts comprising the bolt group are basically the same as those of the Rifle M1903 (fig. 42) but differ slightly in design, and are not all interchangeable.

(9) MAGAZINE SPRING AND FOLLOWER GROUP (figs. 49 and 37). The follower is a sheet metal stamping with a straight ridge running longitudinally on the top side. A portion of the follower near the front (narrow) end is bent downward and inward on both sides to seat the magazine spring, and there is a projection on the rear end to hold it in position. The follower M1903 is a machined piece with an undercut pad on the bottom of the front end to seat the magazine spring, and a pad on the bottom of the rear end to hold it in position (fig. 37). The raised ridge on the top of the follower M1903 has two relief cuts on the left side. As either of these followers may be found assembled in *any* of the rifles covered in this manual, identification is necessary when removing the follower, as explained in the section on disassembly and assembly. Figure 37 shows top and bottom views of both types of followers for identification.

d. U. S. Rifle, Cal. .30, M1903A4 (Snipers).

(1) This rifle was designed for "sniping" and is identical with

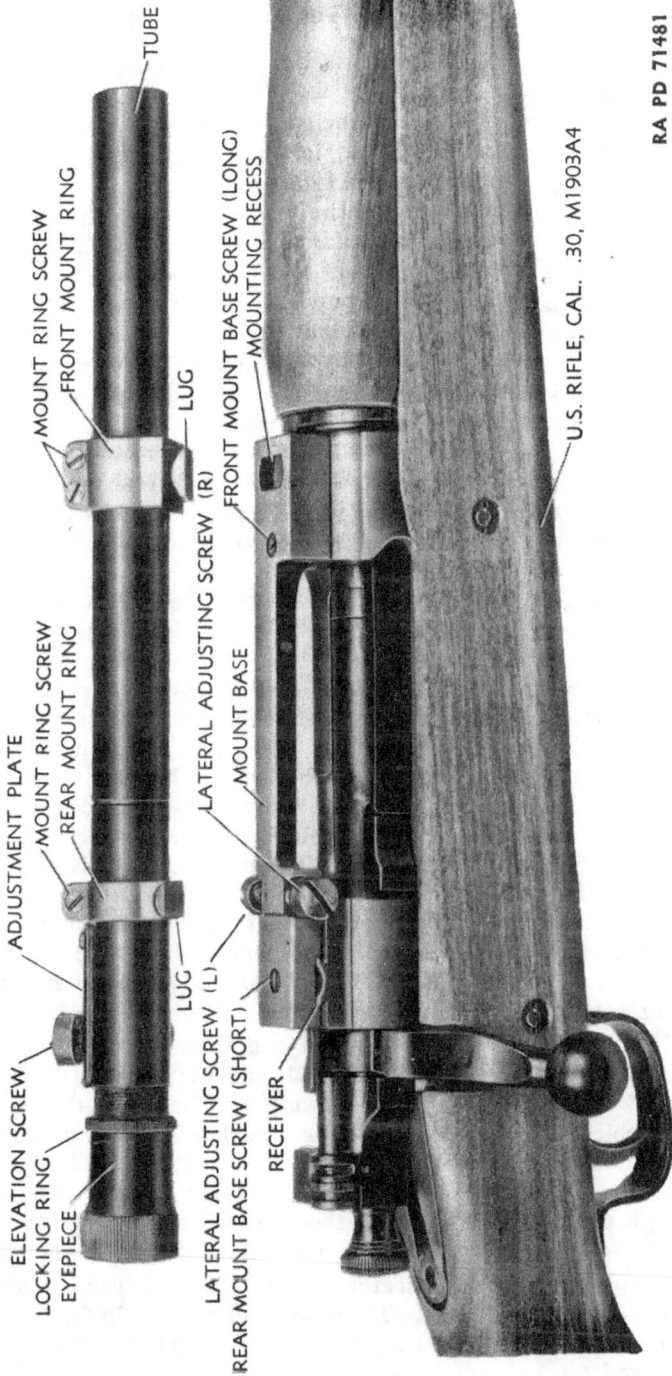

Figure 8 — Telescopic Sight M73B1 (Weaver No. 330 C) Dismounted From Mount Base of U.S. Rifle, cal. .30, M1903A4 (Snipers)

RA PD 71481

ORDNANCE MAINTENANCE — U.S. RIFLES, CAL. .30, M1903, M1903A1, M1903A3 AND M1903A4

the Rifle M1903A3 described in subparagraph c, above, with the following exceptions:

(a) A telescopic sight is mounted to a flat mount base screwed to the top of the receiver (fig. 8) in place of the fixed, wing type rear sight mounted on the Rifle M1903A3 (fig. 7).

(b) The front sight group is entirely removed from the barrel.

(c) The stock assembly is similar to that of the Rifle M1903A1 in that it has a pistol grip and front and rear stock screws and nuts. In addition, it has a bolt handle notch cut into the right side of the stock, to accomodate the modified bolt handle.

(d) The bolt handle curves downward and is cut away on the outside to prevent interference with the telescopic sight when the handle is raised to unlock the bolt or cock the rifle.

(2) Due to interference of the mount base assembled to the top of the receiver for mounting the telescopic sight, and the telescopic sight when mounted, loading this rifle by clip is not practical. Cartridges are inserted into the magazine by hand, one at a time, or the rifle used as a single loader.

(3) At present, the Weaver Commercial Telescopic Sight, No. 330 C (figs. 8 and 67), designated as M73B1, is issued with this rifle. This sight gives a magnification of 2.20 X. The adjusting mechanism is located in the rear end of the sight tube. When mounted, the windage adjusting screw is on the left and the elevation adjusting screw on the top, with respect to the rifle. This sight is furnished with a dust cap assembly for protection of the lenses. It consists of a large and small leather cap connected by a strap. The large cap is placed over the rear (eyepiece) end of the sight and the small cap over the front end. The caps are then turned in opposite directions to take up the slack in the strap by twisting it around the sight tube.

(4) The operation of this rifle and description, care, and adjustment of the telescopic sight are explained in FM 23-10 and TM 9-270, respectively. The mounting of the sight and assembly of the mount base to the rifle are explained in section II of this manual.

e. There are two types of bayonet and three types of scabbards used with the Rifles M1903, M1903A1, and M1903A3. (The Rifle M1903A4 is not equipped with a bayonet.) The one is the Bayonet M1905 which is furnished with either the fabric covered Scabbard M1910 or the plastic Scabbard M3 (figs. 9 and 10). This bayonet has wooden grips and a single edged, 17-inch blade. The other bayonet is the M1 furnished with the plastic Scabbard M7 (fig. 11). This bayonet has composition grips and a single edged, 10-inch blade.

f. The gun sling M1907 (leather) or M1 (web) is used on all four rifles covered in this manual. These slings are shown in figure 12.

NOTE: The slings M1917 (20-18-53) and M1923 (C7791) can also be used.

INTRODUCTION

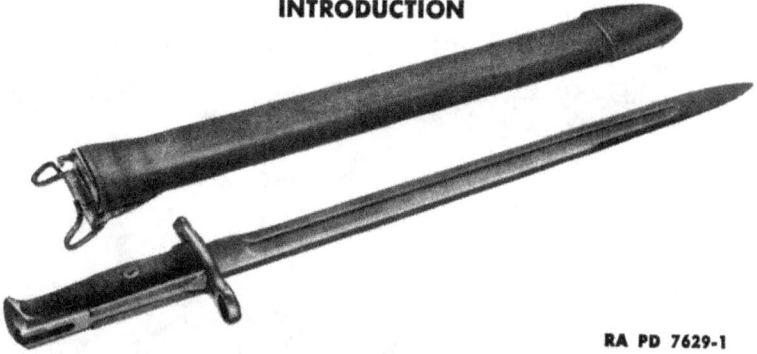

RA PD 7629-1

*Figure 9 — Bayonet M1905 and Bayonet Scabbard M1910
— Assembled View*

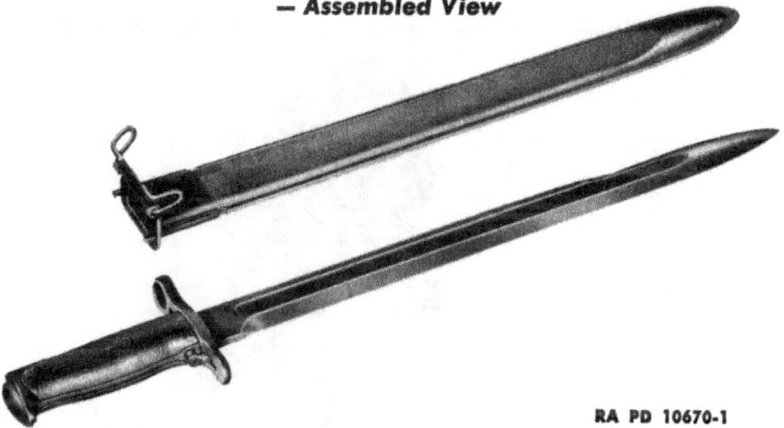

RA PD 10670-1

*Figure 10 — Bayonet M1905 and Bayonet Scabbard M3
— Assembled View*

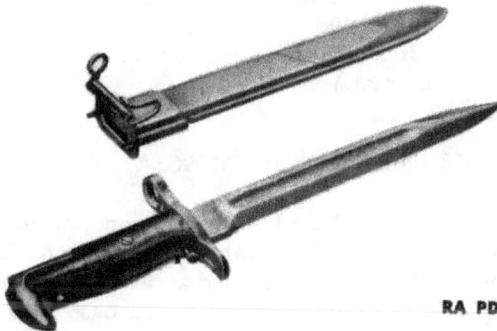

RA PD 84324

*Figure 11 — Bayonet M1 and Bayonet Scabbard M7
— Assembled View*

ORDNANCE MAINTENANCE — U.S. RIFLES, CAL. .30, M1903, M1903A1, M1903A3 AND M1903A4

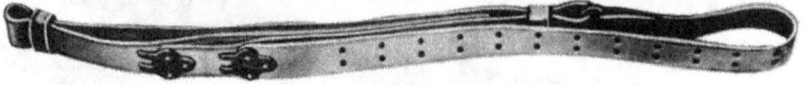

GUN SLING, M1907

GUN SLING, M1

RA PD 22004

Figure 12 — Gun Slings M1907 (20-18-25) and M1 D44058

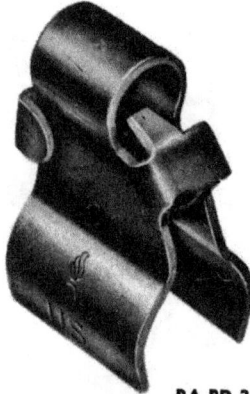

RA PD 21977

Figure 13 — Front Sight Cover C64157

g. The front sight cover C64157 is used to protect the front sight on the Rifles M1903, M1903A1, and M1903A3, and is shown in figure 13. (It is snapped on over the front sight with the sloping portion to the rear.)

4. DATA.

Weight of Rifles M1903 and M1903A1 without bayonet
or gun sling . . . . 8.69 lb
Weight of Rifle M1903A3 without bayonet or gun sling . . . . . . 8.00 lb
Weight of Rifle M1903A4 with Telescopic Sight M73B1
(Weaver No. 330 C) mounted and without gun sling . . . . . . 9.38 lb
Weight of Rifle M1903A4 with mount base only and
without gun sling . . . . 8.88 lb
Weight of gun sling M1907 . . . . 0.50 lb
Weight of Bayonet M1905 . . . . 1.00 lb

INTRODUCTION

Weight of Bayonet M1 . . . . 0.87 lb
Over-all length of rifles without bayonet . . . . 43.46 in.
Over-all length of rifles with Bayonet M1905 . . . . 59.43 in.
Over-all length of rifles with Bayonet M1 . . . . 52.43 in.
Diameter of bore . . . . 0.30 in.
Twist in rifling, uniform right-hand, one turn in . . . . 10.00 in.
Number of grooves in barrel (early design) 4
Number of grooves in barrel (late design) 2
Depth of grooves in barrel (both designs) . . . . 0.004 in.
Sight radius, Rifles M1903 and M1903A1 . . . . 22.14 in.
Sight radius, Rifles M1903 and M1903A1, battle sight set . . 21.56 in.
Sight radius, Rifle M1903A3 (for 200 yd) . . . . 27.8 in.
Sight radius, Rifle M1903A3 (for 800 yd) . . . . 28.4 in.
Maximum graduation of sight (M1903 and M1903A1) . . . . 2,850 yd
Maximum graduation of sight (M1903A3) . . . . 800 yd
Telescopic Sight M73B1 (Weaver No. 330 C):
    Maximum range . . . . 1,250 yd
    Magnification . . . . 2.20 X
    Length (approx.) . . . . 10.50 in.
    Weight with mount rings attached . . . . 0.50 lb
    Parallax adjusted for and beyond . . . . 25 yd
    Graduations of adjusting screws . . . . ¼-min clicks
Weight of CARTRIDGE, ball, cal. .30, M1 (approx.) . . . . 420 grains
Weight of CARTRIDGE, ball, cal. .30, M2 (approx.) . . . . 396 grains
Muzzle velocity, BALL, cal. .30, M1, per second . . . . 2,647 ft
Muzzle velocity, BALL, cal. .30, M2, per second . . . . 2,805 ft
Maximum range, BALL, cal. .30, M1 (approx.) . . . . 5,500 yd
Maximum range, BALL, cal. .30, M2 (approx.) . . . . 3,500 yd
Chamber pressure (approx.):
    Ammunition M1, per square inch (mean) . . . . 48,000 lb
    Ammunition M2, per square inch (mean) . . . . 50,000 lb
Shipping weight of 10 Rifles, M1903, M1903A1, and
M1903A3 packed in standard container . . . . 150.00 lb
Shipping weight of 10 M1903A4 Rifles, with Telescopic
Sight M73B1 (Weaver No. 330 C) in standard
container . . . . 151.00 lb
Shipping weight of 100 M1905 Bayonets, packed in
wood box . . . . 147.00 lb
Shipping weight of 100 M1 Bayonets, packed in wood box . . 131.00 lb
Shipping weight of 250 M1910 Bayonet Scabbards, packed
in wood box . . . . 145.00 lb
Shipping weight of 200 M3 Bayonet Scabbards, packed in
wood box . . . . 154.00 lb
Shipping weight of 288 M7 Bayonet Scabbards, packed in
wood box . . . . 155.00 lb
    NOTE: 7,000 grains equal 1 pound avoirdupois measure.

ORDNANCE MAINTENANCE — U.S. RIFLES, CAL. .30,
M1903, M1903A1, M1903A3 AND M1903A4

5. OPERATION AND FUNCTIONING (figs. 14 and 15).

a. **General.** The manual operation and the mechanical function-ing of the moving parts and mechanisms of the rifle are so closely related that they are described together in the order of their perform-ance. For a description of the use of this rifle by line organizations, covering operation, functioning, care, and the proper nomenclature of the parts, refer to FM 23-10 and SNL B-3.

b. **Bolt Group Mechanism.**

(1) DESCRIPTION. The bolt group mechanism, commonly referred to as the bolt, consists of the bolt assembly, bolt sleeve assembly, extractor, safety lock assembly, firing pin assembly, firing pin sleeve, striker, and mainspring. The components of the bolt group are shown in figures 42 and 43.

(a) Bolt Assembly. The bolt assembly consists of the bolt and the extractor collar (figs. 17 and 18). The bolt moves backward and for-ward and rotates in the well of the receiver (fig. 27). It pushes a cartridge from the magazine, or one placed by hand in front of it, into the chamber and supports the head of the cartridge during firing. The bolt has two locking lugs formed at the front end which sustain the shock of the discharge by engagement with the locking shoulders on the receiver (fig. 25). The upper locking lug is slotted to allow the passage of the point of the ejector (fig. 17). Two small circular notches are located on the left side of the slotted lug (fig. 16). These notches engage the bolt stop pin in either single or magazine loading and retain the bolt in place in the open position. (In some bolts these notches are absent, as explained in paragraph 43 i.) A safety lug (fig. 17) is formed midway on the bolt which comes into play only in the event of the locking lugs yielding under pressure at discharge.

(b) Bolt Sleeve Assembly (figs. 20 and 21). The bolt sleeve unites the parts of the bolt group mechanism, and its rotation with the bolt is prevented by the lugs on its sides coming in contact with the receiver (fig. 14). It has a groove through which the cocking piece lug extends to enter the cocking piece groove in the receiver. The bolt sleeve lock (fig. 20) is provided to prevent accidental turning of the bolt sleeve when the bolt is drawn back.

(c) Extractor. The hook at the front end of the extractor (fig. 16) engages in the extracting groove of the cartridge case and retains the head of the case in the countersink of the bolt until the case is ejected (fig. 30).

(d) Safety Lock Assembly (figs. 22 and 23). The safety lock when turned to the left in the "READY" position, is inoperative; when turned to the right in the "SAFE" position (which can only be done when the rifle is cocked), the point of the spindle (fig. 20) enters its notch in the bolt (fig. 19) and locks the bolt; at the same time its

INTRODUCTION

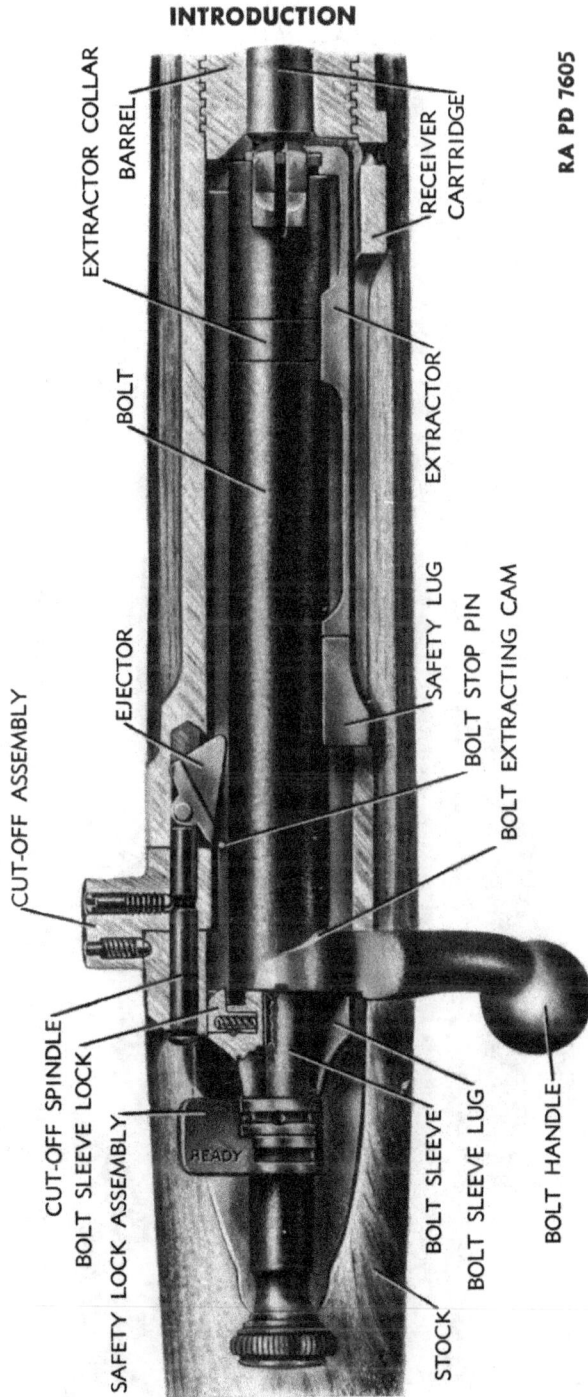

RA PD 7605

EXTRACTOR COLLAR

BARREL

RECEIVER

CARTRIDGE

BOLT

EXTRACTOR

SAFETY LUG

BOLT STOP PIN

BOLT EXTRACTING CAM

EJECTOR

CUT-OFF ASSEMBLY

CUT-OFF SPINDLE

BOLT SLEEVE LOCK

SAFETY LOCK ASSEMBLY

READY

BOLT SLEEVE

BOLT SLEEVE LUG

STOCK

BOLT HANDLE

Figure 14 — U.S. Rifle, cal. .30, M1903A1 — Section Through Receiver — Plan View

ORDNANCE MAINTENANCE — U.S. RIFLES, CAL. .30,
M1903, M1903A1, M1903A3 AND M1903A4

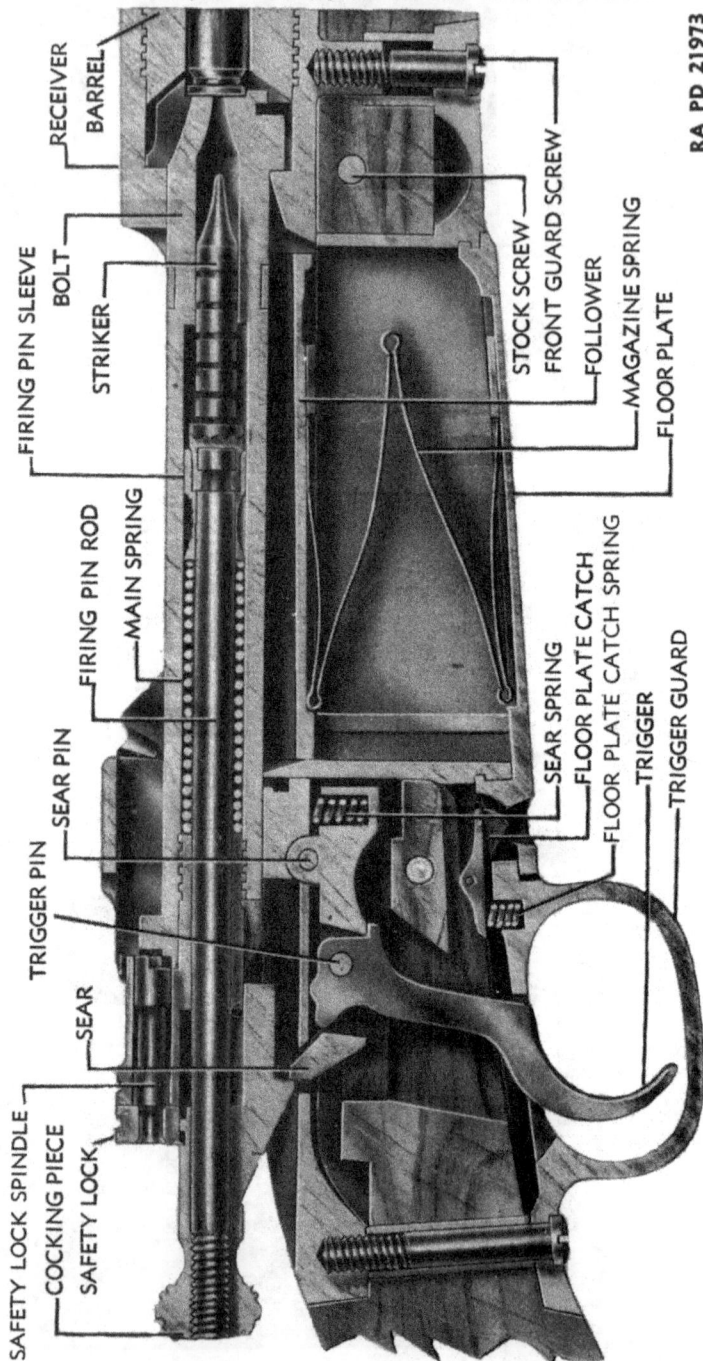

RA PD 21973

RECEIVER

BARREL

FIRING PIN SLEEVE

BOLT

STRIKER

FIRING PIN ROD

MAIN SPRING

SEAR PIN

TRIGGER PIN

SEAR

SAFETY LOCK SPINDLE

COCKING PIECE

SAFETY LOCK

STOCK SCREW

FRONT GUARD SCREW

FOLLOWER

MAGAZINE SPRING

FLOOR PLATE

SEAR SPRING

FLOOR PLATE CATCH

FLOOR PLATE CATCH SPRING

TRIGGER

TRIGGER GUARD

Figure 15 — U.S. Rifle, cal. .30, M1903A1 — Section Through Receiver — Vertical View

INTRODUCTION

cam forces the cocking piece slightly to the rear out of contact with the sear and locks the firing pin.

(e) Firing Pin Assembly. The firing pin assembly consists of the cocking piece and the firing pin rod (fig. 24). When the rifle is cocked, the mainspring will remain compressed as long as the sear nose is retained in the sear notch of the cocking piece. The length of the firing pin rod is so adjusted that when the front end of the cocking piece bears against the interior shoulder of the bolt sleeve, the striker will project the proper distance beyond the face of the bolt.

(f) Firing Pin Sleeve. The firing pin sleeve fits over the front end of the firing pin rod and the rear end of the striker, covering the joint hole and preventing accidental separation of the firing pin rod and striker (fig. 15). Its rear end forms the front bearing of the mainspring.

(g) Striker. The striker has a joint hole formed on its rear end by which it is secured to the firing pin rod (fig. 15). When the mainspring forces the firing pin assembly forward, the point of the striker strikes the primer of the cartridge held in the chamber.

(h) Mainspring. The mainspring is mounted on the firing pin rod; the front end resting against the rear face of the firing pin sleeve and the rear end resting against the barrel of the bolt sleeve (fig. 15). When the sear releases the cocking piece, the mainspring drives the firing pin and the striker forward.

(2) OPENING THE BOLT.

(a) The bolt is opened by raising the bolt handle until it comes in contact with the left side of the receiver and pulling directly to the rear until the upper locking lug strikes the cut-off.

(b) Raising the bolt handle rotates the bolt and separates the locking lugs from their seats on the locking shoulders in the receiver (fig. 25) with which they have been brought into close contact by the pressure of the powder gases. This rotation causes the cocking cam of the bolt (fig. 16) to force the firing pin to the rear, drawing the point of the striker into the bolt, rotation of the firing pin being prevented by the lug on the cocking piece projecting through the slot in the bolt sleeve into its groove in the receiver (fig. 27). As the bolt sleeve remains longitudinally stationary with reference to the bolt, this rearward motion of the firing pin and consequently of the striker will start the compression of the mainspring, since the rear end of the mainspring bears against the front end of the barrel of the bolt sleeve and its front end against the rear end of the firing pin sleeve (fig. 15).

(c) When the bolt handle strikes the receiver, the locking lugs have been disengaged, the firing pin has been forced to the rear until the sear notch of the cocking piece has passed the sear nose (fig. 26), the cocking piece nose (fig. 24) has entered the cock notch in the rear end of the bolt (fig. 19), the bolt sleeve lock (fig. 20) has engaged its notch in the bolt (fig. 19), and the mainspring has been almost

ORDNANCE MAINTENANCE — U.S. RIFLES, CAL. .30,
M1903, M1903A1, M1903A3 AND M1903A4

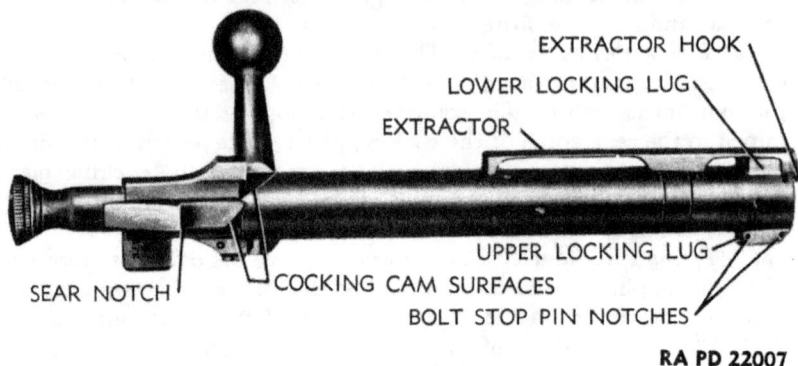

EXTRACTOR HOOK

LOWER LOCKING LUG

EXTRACTOR

UPPER LOCKING LUG

SEAR NOTCH

COCKING CAM SURFACES

BOLT STOP PIN NOTCHES

RA PD 22007

Figure 16 — Bolt Group Assembled

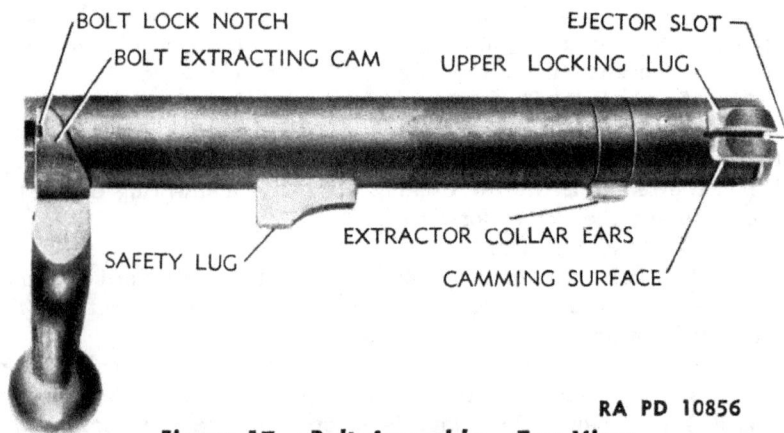

BOLT LOCK NOTCH

BOLT EXTRACTING CAM

EJECTOR SLOT

UPPER LOCKING LUG

SAFETY LUG

EXTRACTOR COLLAR EARS

CAMMING SURFACE

RA PD 10856

Figure 17 — Bolt Assembly — Top View

entirely compressed. During the rotation of the bolt, a rearward motion has been imparted to it by its extracting cam (fig. 14) coming in contact with the extracting cam of the receiver (fig. 28) so that the cartridge case will be started from the chamber. (In figure 26 the extracting cam of the receiver is hidden from view by the extracting cam of the bolt.) The bolt is then drawn directly to the rear, the parts being retained in position by the cocking piece nose remaining in the cock notch and locked by the bolt sleeve lock engaging its notch in the bolt.

(*d*) Just before the bolt is drawn fully to the rear, the upper locking lug strikes the heel of the ejector, throwing its point suddenly to the right in the lug slot (fig. 33). As the bolt moves fully to the rear, the rear face of the cartridge case strikes against the ejector point and the case is ejected slightly upward and to the right from the receiver.

INTRODUCTION

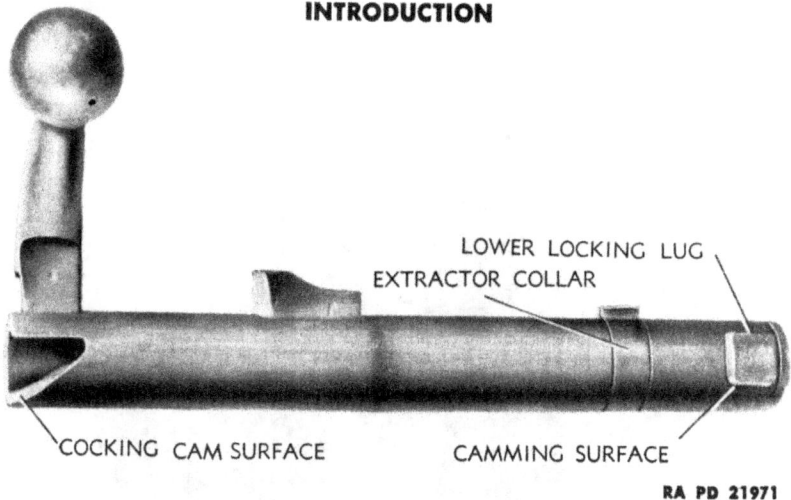

LOWER LOCKING LUG

EXTRACTOR COLLAR

COCKING CAM SURFACE   CAMMING SURFACE

RA PD 21971

Figure 18 — Bolt Assembly — Bottom View

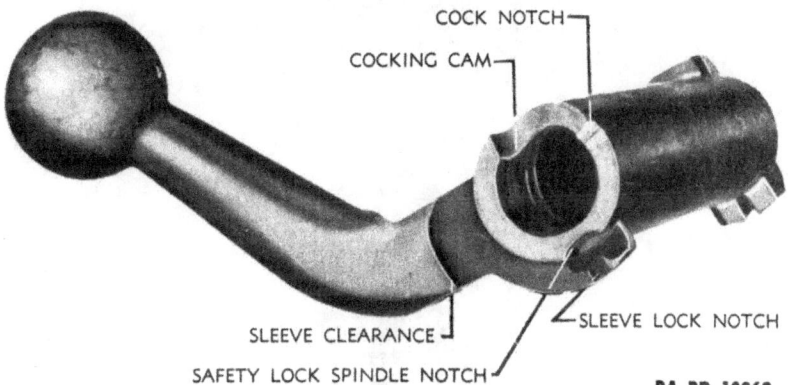

COCK NOTCH

COCKING CAM

SLEEVE CLEARANCE   SLEEVE LOCK NOTCH

SAFETY LOCK SPINDLE NOTCH

RA PD 10869

Figure 19 — Bolt Assembly — Rear View

(3) CLOSING THE BOLT.

(a) The bolt is closed by pushing the bolt handle forward until the extracting cam on the bolt bears against the extracting cam on the receiver. The bolt is unlocked from the bolt sleeve by the bolt sleeve lock striking the bridge of the receiver. The bolt handle is then turned down.

(b) As the bolt handle is turned down, the cams of the locking lugs (figs. 17 and 18) bear against the locking shoulders in the receiver (fig. 25), and the bolt is forced slightly forward into its closed position with the locking lugs resting against the lug seats. As all movement of the firing pin is prevented by the sear nose engaging the sear notch of the cocking piece (fig. 26), this forward movement of the

ORDNANCE MAINTENANCE — U.S. RIFLES, CAL. .30,
M1903, M1903A1, M1903A3 AND M1903A4

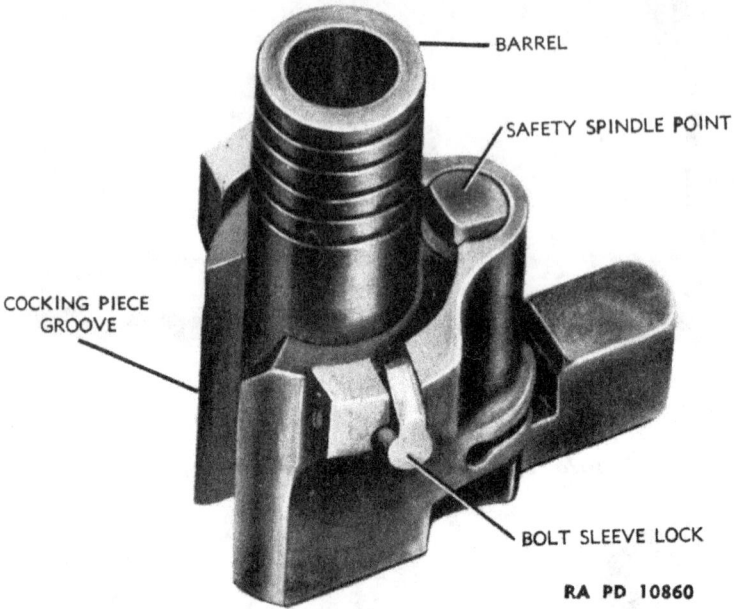

BARREL

SAFETY SPINDLE POINT

COCKING PIECE
GROOVE

BOLT SLEEVE LOCK

RA PD 10860

Figure 20 — Bolt Sleeve Assembly — Front View

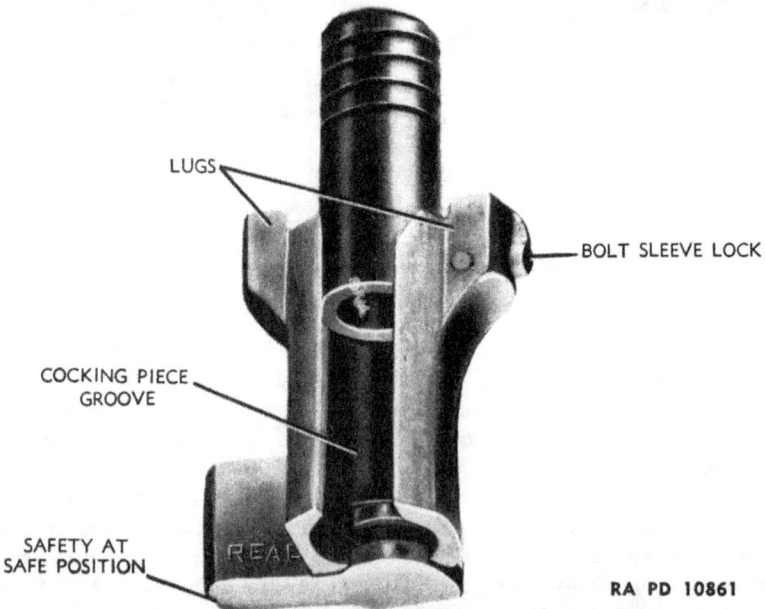

LUGS

BOLT SLEEVE LOCK

COCKING PIECE
GROOVE

SAFETY AT
SAFE POSITION

RA PD 10861

Figure 21 — Bolt Sleeve Assembly — Rear View

SAFETY AT SAFE RIFLE COCKED

SAFETY CAMS

CUT-OFF AT OFF POSITION

RA PD 10854

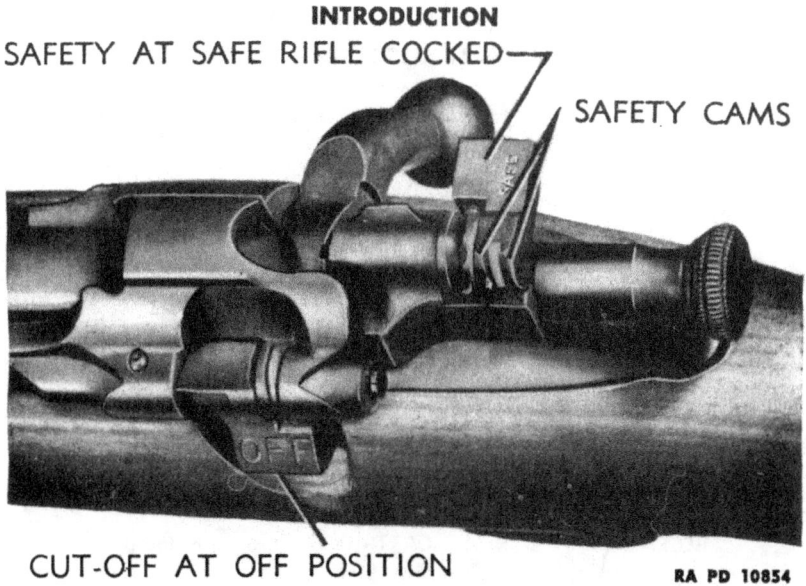

Figure 22 — Safety at "SAFE" and Cut-off at "OFF"

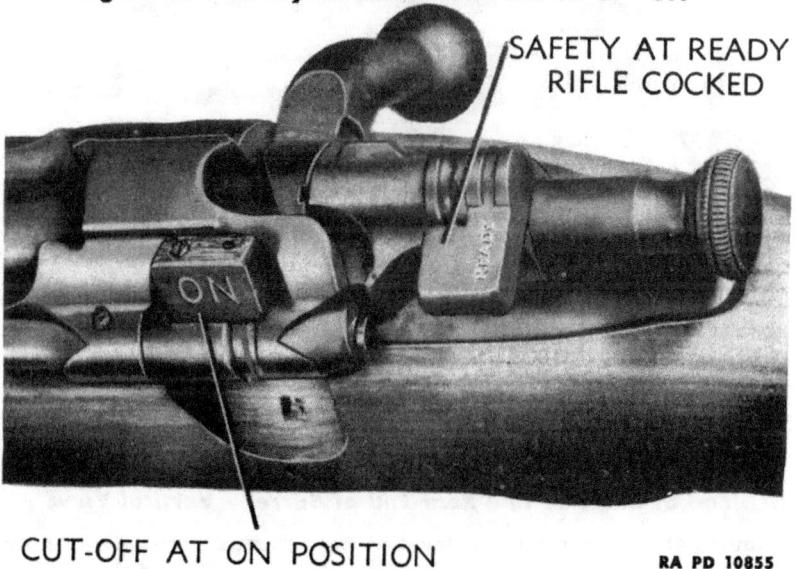

SAFETY AT READY
RIFLE COCKED

CUT-OFF AT ON POSITION

RA PD 10855

Figure 23 — Safety at "READY" and Cut-off at "ON"

bolt completes the compression of the mainspring, seats the cartridge in the chamber, and in single loading forces the hook of the extractor into the groove of the cartridge case.

(c) In loading from the magazine, the hook of the extractor,

ORDNANCE MAINTENANCE — U.S. RIFLES, CAL. .30,
M1903, M1903A1, M1903A3 AND M1903A4

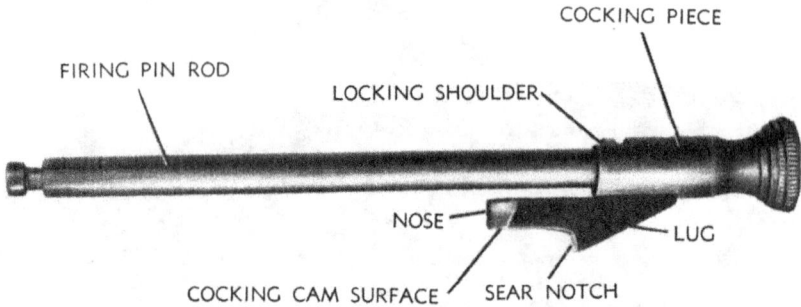

FIRING PIN ROD

COCKING PIECE

LOCKING SHOULDER

NOSE

LUG

COCKING CAM SURFACE

SEAR NOTCH

RA PD 10859

Figure 24 — Firing Pin Assembly

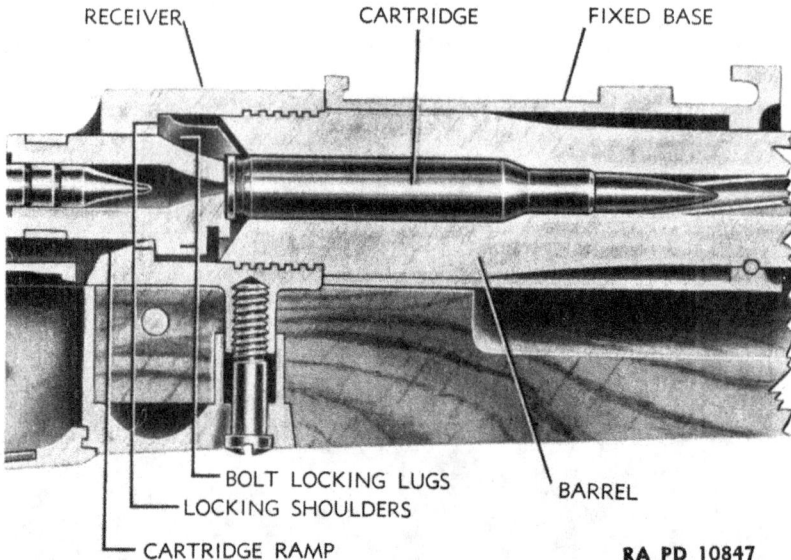

RECEIVER

CARTRIDGE

FIXED BASE

BOLT LOCKING LUGS
LOCKING SHOULDERS

BARREL

CARTRIDGE RAMP

RA PD 10847

Figure 25 — Camming System A — Section Through Forward
End of Receiver and Rear End of Barrel — Vertical View

rounded at its lower edge, engages in the extracting groove of the top
cartridge as it rises from the magazine under the action of the follower
and magazine spring (fig. 29). The cartridge can not come out of
magazine well until pushed forward by the bolt. This prevents double
feeding. The position occupied by the bolt and cartridge is shown in
figures 14 and 15.

(4) CAMMING SYSTEM. It will be noted that in this type of bolt
mechanism, the compression of the mainspring, the seating of the car-

INTRODUCTION

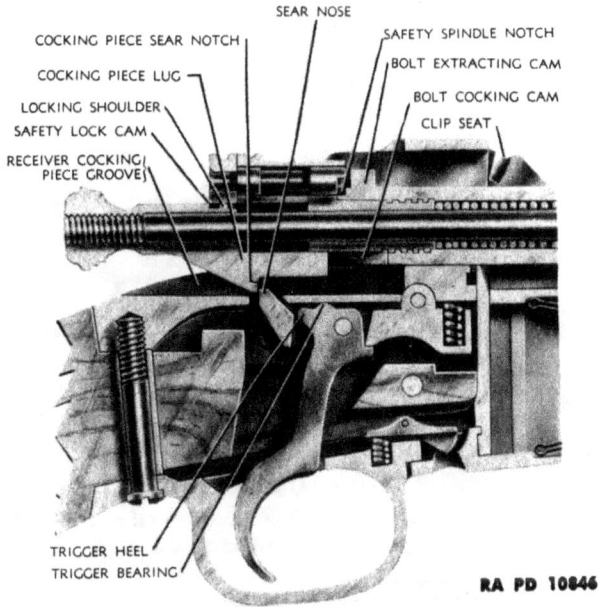

Figure 26 — Camming System B — Section Through
Rear End of Receiver — Vertical View

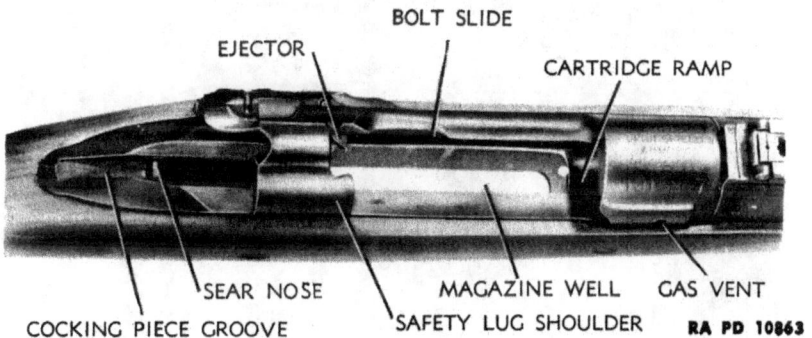

Figure 27 — Receiver — Bolt and Magazine Mechanism
Removed — Top View

tridge in the chamber, and the starting of the empty case from the chamber are entirely done by the action of cams.

c. Magazine Mechanism.

(1) DESCRIPTION. The magazine mechanism for the M1903 and M1903A1 Rifles, consists of the floor plate, follower, and magazine spring. The components are shown in figure 47. The functioning of the magazine mechanism is controlled by the position of the cut-off on the receiver (figs. 22 and 23), which limits the movement of the

ORDNANCE MAINTENANCE — U.S. RIFLES, CAL. .30, M1903, M1903A1, M1903A3 AND M1903A4

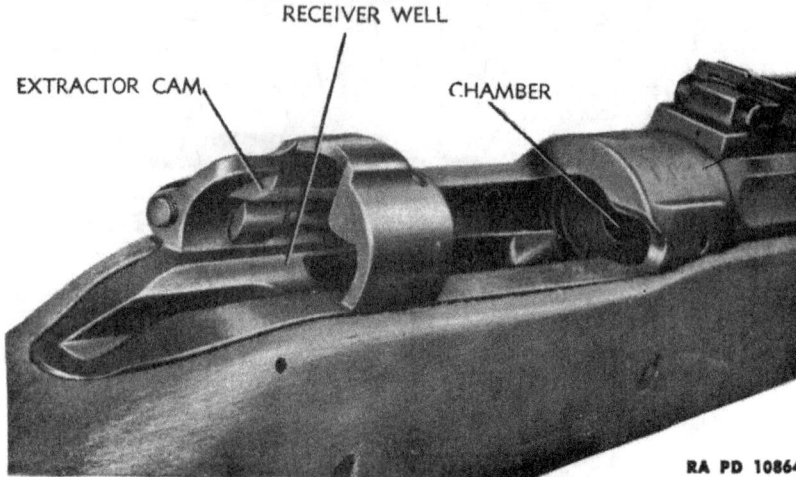

RECEIVER WELL

EXTRACTOR CAM

CHAMBER

RA PD 10864

Figure 28 — Receiver — Bolt Removed — Showing Location of Extractor Cam

RA PD 10875

Figure 29 — Cartridge Being Pushed Into Chamber by Bolt

bolt (figs. 31 and 32). The floor plate supports the magazine spring which forces the follower upward. When feeding cartridges from the magazine (fig. 29), the follower raises the cartridges in the magazine so that the top cartridge projects through the magazine opening in the receiver far enough to be caught by the bolt on its forward movement.

(2) CHARGING MAGAZINE. With cut-off turned up showing "ON," and the bolt drawn fully to the rear, cartridges are inserted from a

INTRODUCTION

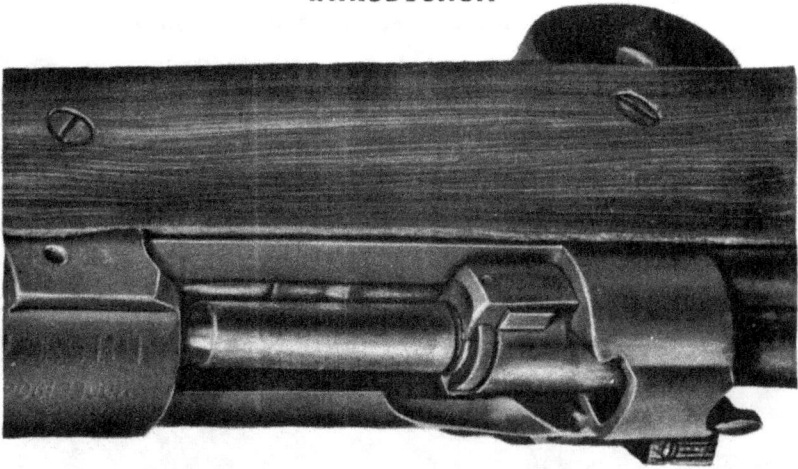

Figure 30 — Extractor Holding Cartridge Head and Cartridge Being Extracted From Chamber

clip or from the hand, and the bolt closed. When charging the magazine from a clip, either end of a loaded clip is placed in its seat in the receiver and the cartridges pressed down into the magazine with the thumb until the top cartridge is caught by the right edge of the receiver. Pushing the bolt forward after charging the magazine ejects the clip. The cartridge ramp (fig. 27) guides the bullet and cartridge case into the chamber. The magazine can be filled, if partly filled, by inserting cartridges one by one. (This latter type of loading is necessary for the Rifle M1903A4 with telescopic sight mounted.)

(3) CUT-OFF AT "OFF." When the cut-off is turned down, the magazine is "OFF." The bolt cannot be drawn fully back, and its front end, projecting over the rear end of the upper cartridge, holds it down in the magazine below the action of the bolt (fig. 31). The magazine mechanism then remains inoperative, and the rifle can be used as a single-loader, the cartridges in the magazine being held in reserve. The rifle can readily be used as a single-loader with the magazine empty.

(4) CUT-OFF AT "ON." When the cut-off is turned up, the magazine is "ON." The bolt can be drawn fully to the rear, permitting the top cartridge to rise high enough to be caught by the bolt in its forward movement (fig. 32). As the bolt is closed, this cartridge is pushed forward into the chamber (fig. 29), being held up during its passage by the pressure of those below. The last one in the magazine is held up by the follower, the rib of which directs it into the chamber.

(5) ACTION OF FOLLOWER. In magazine fire, after the last cartridge has been fired and the bolt drawn fully to the rear, the follower

ORDNANCE MAINTENANCE — U.S. RIFLES, CAL. .30,
M1903, M1903A1, M1903A3 AND M1903A4

RA PD 10867

Figure 31 — Cartridges in Magazine — Cut-off at "OFF"

RA PD 10866

Figure 32 — Cartridges in Magazine — Cut-off at "ON"

INTRODUCTION

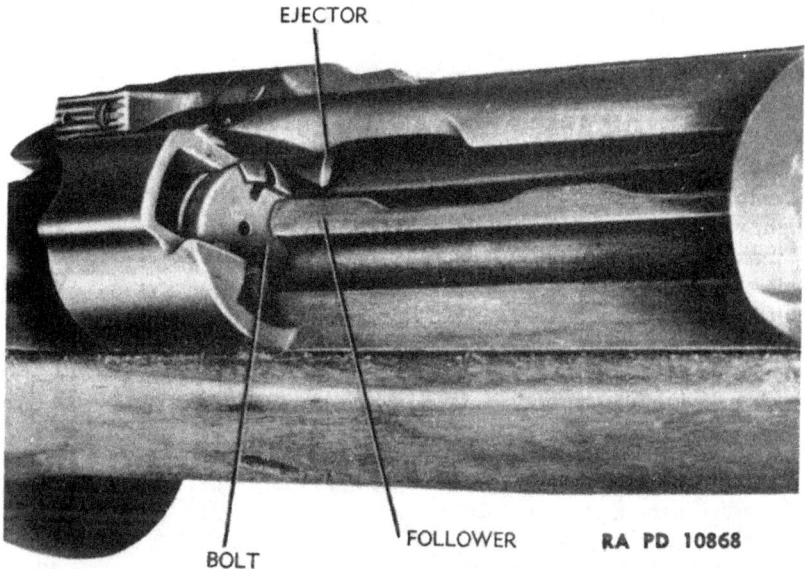

*Figure 33 — Position of Follower — Magazine Empty —
Cut-off at "ON"*

rises and holds the bolt open to show that the magazine is empty (fig. 33).

d. **Cocking the Rifle.** The rifle may be cocked either by raising the bolt handle until it strikes the left side of the receiver and then immediately turning it down, or by pulling the cocking piece (fig. 15) directly to the rear until the sear notch on the cocking piece has passed the sear nose.

e. **Firing the Rifle.** The rifle is fired by drawing the finger piece of the trigger to the rear until contact with the receiver is transferred from the normal bearing surface to the heel (fig. 26), which takes up the slack. The action of the trigger is then continued until the sear nose is withdrawn from in front of the cocking piece or sear notch. In firing, unless the bolt handle is turned fully down, the cam on the cocking piece will strike the cocking cam on the bolt, and the energy of the mainspring will be expended in closing the bolt instead of on the primer through the medium of the striker. This prevents the possibility of a cartridge being fired before the bolt is fully closed.

ORDNANCE MAINTENANCE — U.S. RIFLES, CAL. .30,
M1903, M1903A1, M1903A3 AND M1903A4

Section II
DISASSEMBLY AND ASSEMBLY

6. GENERAL.

a. As the four rifles covered in this manual are basically the same, disassembly and assembly are explained for the basic Rifles M1903 and M1903A1. Variations in procedure for the Rifles M1903A3 and M1903A4 are explained as they occur in the various groups.

b. For convenience, the parts of the rifle have been divided into "groups" and "assemblies." A group is a number of parts which function together in the rifle and which are closely related to each other. An assembly consists of two or more parts which are either permanently or semipermanently assembled and should not ordinarily be taken apart. The groups, assemblies, and individual parts are listed in the following paragraphs in the order in which they would be taken from the rifle.

c. Disassembly will be considered under two general heads:

(1) Removal of groups from the rifle to the extent necessary to perform ordinary cleaning.

(2) Detailed disassembly covering the removal of all components of each group.

d. The tools for use in removal of groups from the rifle and in disassembling and assembling groups and assemblies are those provided

DISASSEMBLY AND ASSEMBLY

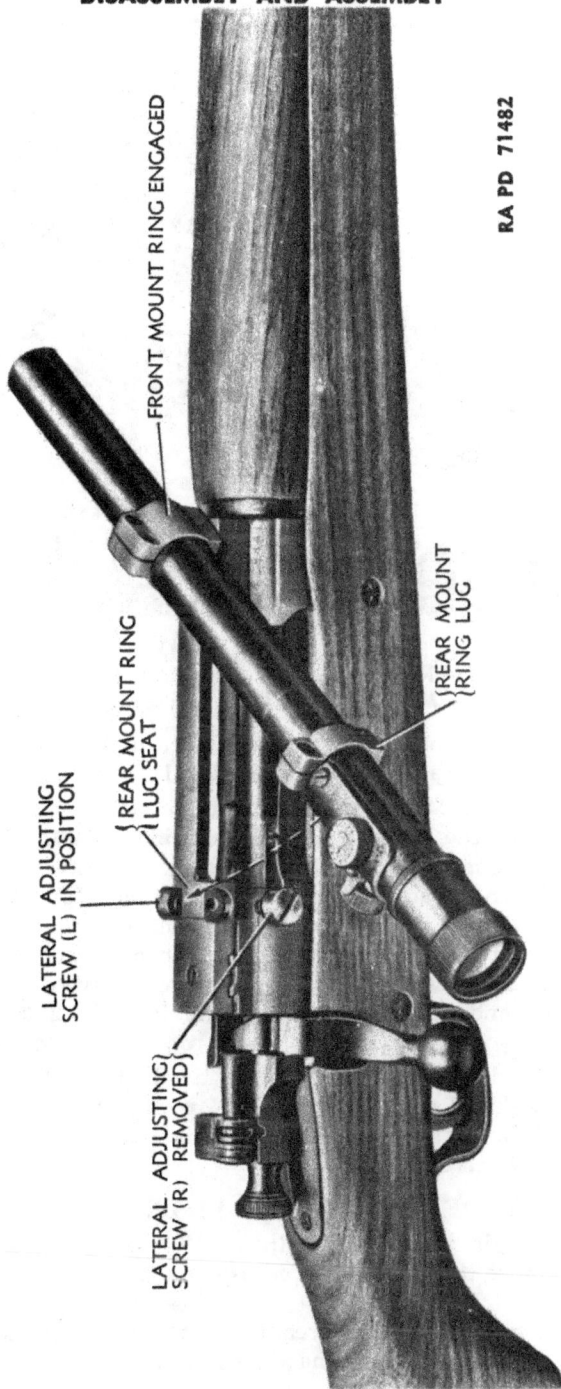

RA PD 71482

FRONT MOUNT RING ENGAGED

REAR MOUNT
RING LUG

REAR MOUNT RING
LUG SEAT

LATERAL ADJUSTING
SCREW (L) IN POSITION

LATERAL ADJUSTING
SCREW (R) REMOVED

Figure 34 — Telescopic Sight M73B1 (Weaver No. 330 C) Partially Dismounted From
U.S. Rifle, cal. .30, M1903A4

ORDNANCE MAINTENANCE — U.S. RIFLES, CAL. .30,
M1903, M1903A1, M1903A3 AND M1903A4

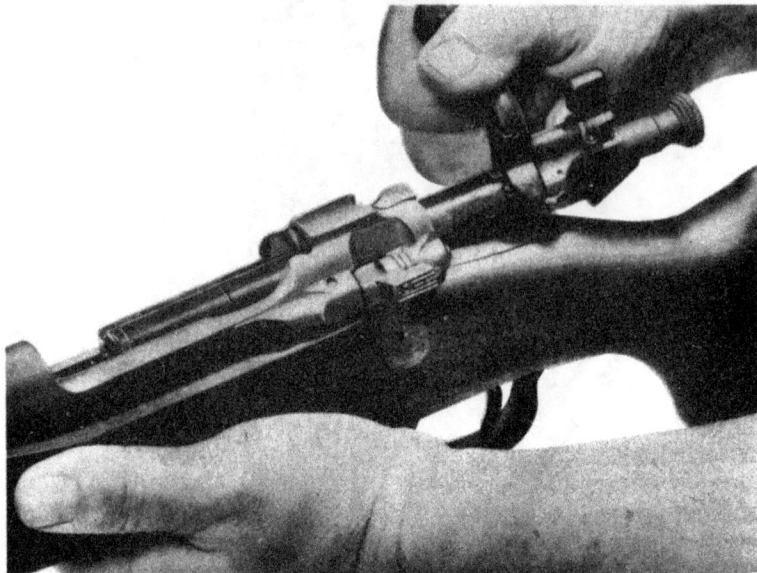

RA PD 7606

*Figure 35 — Removing Bolt From U.S. Rifle, cal. .30,
M1903A1 (or Other Models)*

as company accessories. They are also carried on the small arms
repair truck and are listed in SNL B-3 and SNL B-20.

e. The telescopic sight with mount rings attached (fig. 8) should be
removed from the mount base of the Rifle M1903A4 before the
remaining groups are removed. This is to avoid possible damage to
the sight which is very delicate in construction. Likewise, the sight
should be mounted to the rifle only after all other groups have been
assembled and installed. Dismounting and mounting the telescopic
sight as well as disassembly and assembly are explained in this manual.
Adjustments and care are covered in detail in TM 9-270.

f. The rear sight assembly of the M1903 and M1903A1 Rifles is
mounted on the barrel while that of the Rifle M1903A3 and the
telescopic sight of the Rifle M1903A4 is mounted on the receiver.
Disassembly and assembly of these sights are covered in the group
in which they occur.

7. REMOVAL OF GROUPS FROM RIFLE.

a. Telescopic Sight Group, Rifle M1903A4.

(1) Remove the *right* lateral adjusting screw from the mount base
(fig. 34).

(2) Grasp the sight just to rear of front mount ring and swing rear
end away from receiver (bolt handle side) until sight is at right angles

36

DISASSEMBLY AND ASSEMBLY

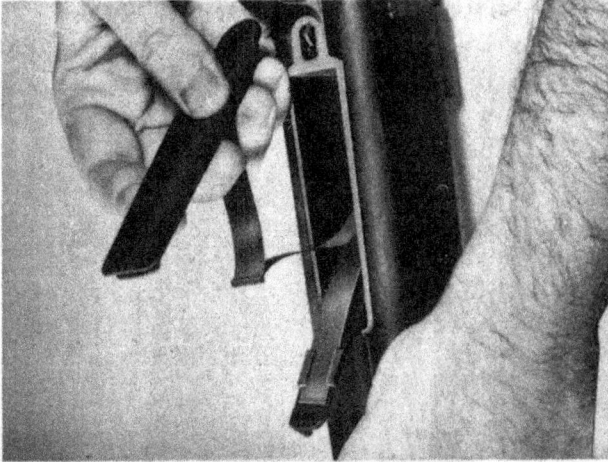

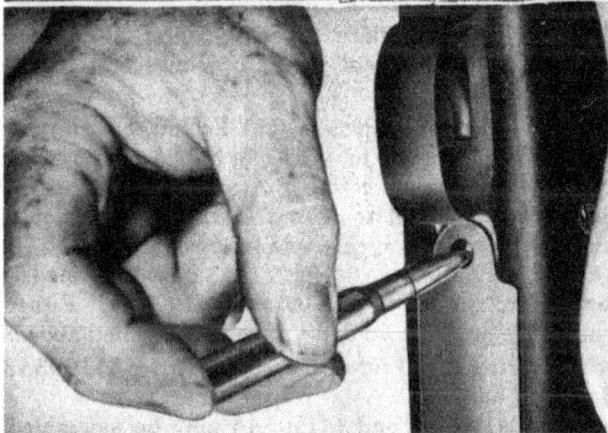

A. DEPRESSING FLOOR PLATE   RA PD 7607   B. FLOOR PLATE RELEASED   RA PD 7608   C. REMOVING FLOOR PLATE MAGAZINE SPRING AND FOLLOWER   RA PD 7609

Figure 36 — Removing Floor Plate, Magazine Spring and Follower From U.S. Rifle, cal. .30, M1903A1 (or M1903)

ORDNANCE MAINTENANCE — U.S. RIFLES, CAL. .30,
M1903, M1903A1, M1903A3 AND M1903A4

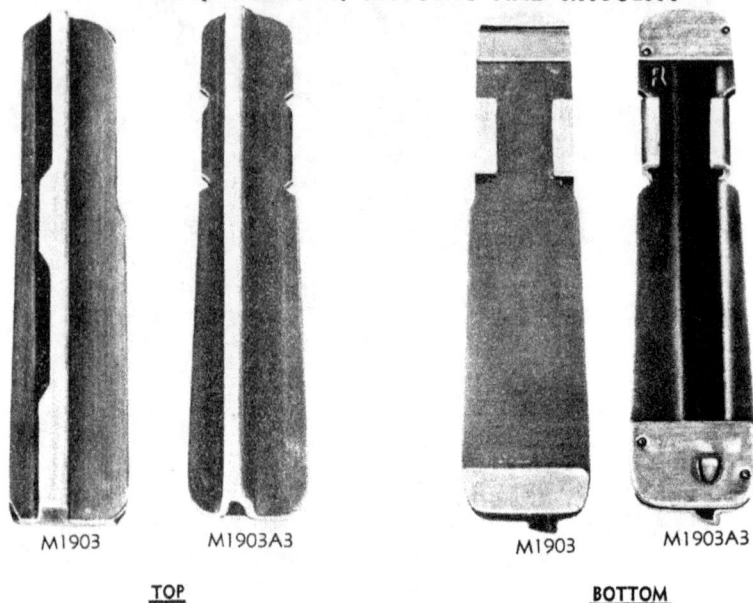

M1903   M1903A3   M1903   M1903A3

TOP   BOTTOM

RA PD 84306

Figure 37 — Followers of M1903 and M1903A3 Types
— Top and Bottom Views

to receiver (fig. 34 shows sight partially dismounted).

(3) Lift sight straight up from mount base.

(4) Thread *right* lateral adjusting screw into mount base to prevent loss.

CAUTION: Do not disturb *left* lateral adjusting screw, as it is staked in position for alinement of sight.

b. **Bolt Group** (fig. 35). Place cut-off at center notch, cock rifle, and turn safety lock to a vertical position. Raise bolt handle and draw out bolt to rear.

c. **Floor Plate, Magazine Spring, and Follower Group, Rifles M1903 and M1903A1** (fig. 36). With the bullet end of a cartridge or pin drift, press on floor plate catch (through hole in floor plate) at the same time drawing bullet to rear; this releases the floor plate. Remove floor plate, magazine spring, and follower together.

NOTE: Either the M1903 or the M1903A3 type follower (fig. 37) may be assembled to the Rifles M1903 and M1903A1. Either type follower should be removed from these rifles as explained above.

d. **Magazine Spring and Follower Group, Rifles M1903A3 and M1903A4** (figs. 37 and 49).

(1) The Rifles M1903A3 and M1903A4 may be assembled with

DISASSEMBLY AND ASSEMBLY

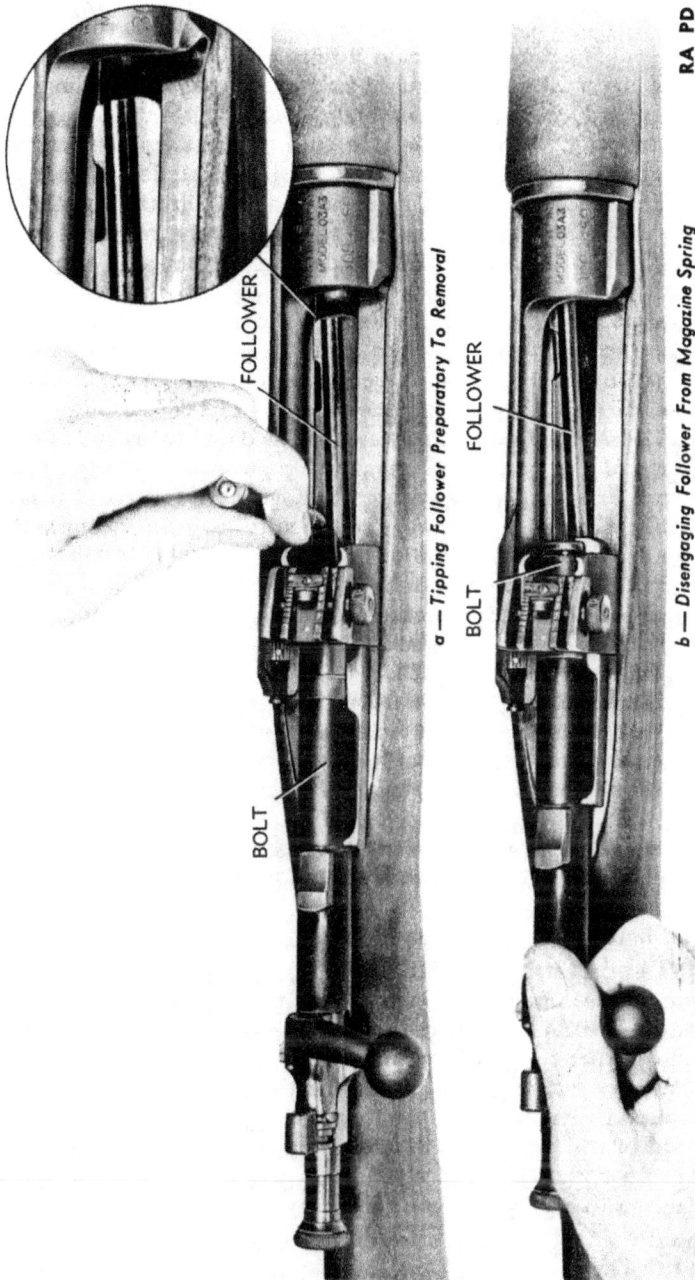

Figure 38 — Removing Magazine Spring and M1903A3 Type Follower From Rifle M1903A3

RA PD 79916

a — Tipping Follower Preparatory To Removal

b — Disengaging Follower From Magazine Spring

FOLLOWER

FOLLOWER

BOLT

BOLT

ORDNANCE MAINTENANCE — U.S. RIFLES, CAL. .30, M1903, M1903A1, M1903A3 AND M1903A4

either the M1903A3 or the M1903 type follower (fig. 37), as explained in paragraph 3 c (9). The M1903 type magazine spring and follower can only be removed from the Rifles M1903A3 and M1903A4 by removing the front and rear guard screws (fig. 49) and pulling out the trigger guard magazine assembly together with the magazine spring and follower. (Unless the rifle is to be disassembled further, the trigger guard magazine assembly should be reinstalled at once, as the guard screws hold the barrel, receiver, and stock groups together.)

(2) The M1903A3 type follower (fig. 37) can be removed from the Rifles M1903A3 and M1903A4 as described above. It also may be removed from the Rifle M1903A3 without removing the trigger guard magazine assembly or bolt assembly as described below. This latter method is not practical in the case of the Rifle M1903A4 due to interference of the mount base assembled to the top of the receiver. The method of removal described below should never be attempted when the M1903 type follower is assembled, as damage to the follower and chamber of the barrel will result. To remove M1903A3 type follower from Rifle M1903A3 without removing trigger guard magazine assembly, proceed as follows, else difficulty may be encountered.

(a) Position rifle with muzzle to left.

(b) Set cut-off at "ON" position.

(c) Unlock and pull bolt to extreme rearward position.

(d) Insert nose of bullet directly in front of ejector and against left side of follower rib (a, fig. 38).

(e) Tip rear of follower downward and toward right side of receiver until front left side of follower emerges through magazine slot at front of receiver to rest upon lip of receiver.

(f) Move bolt forward slowly against rear face of follower to disengage follower from magazine spring (b, fig. 38). (It may be necessary to pry up rear end of follower to engage bolt.)

CAUTION: Do not allow front end of follower to strike mouth of chamber.

(g) Pull bolt to rear and remove follower and magazine spring.

8. REINSTALLATION OF GROUPS IN RIFLE.

a. **Floor Plate, Magazine Spring, and Follower Group, Rifles M1903 and M1903A1.** Insert floor plate, magazine spring, and follower group (either type follower, fig. 37) into the magazine, follower first with narrow end forward. Place the tenon on the front end of the floor plate in its recess in the magazine; then place the lug on the rear end of the floor plate in its slot in the trigger guard. Press rear end of floor plate forward and inward at the same time, forcing floor plate into its seat in trigger guard.

b. **Magazine Spring and Follower Group, Rifles M1903A3 and M1903A4.** These rifles may be assembled with either the M1903

DISASSEMBLY AND ASSEMBLY

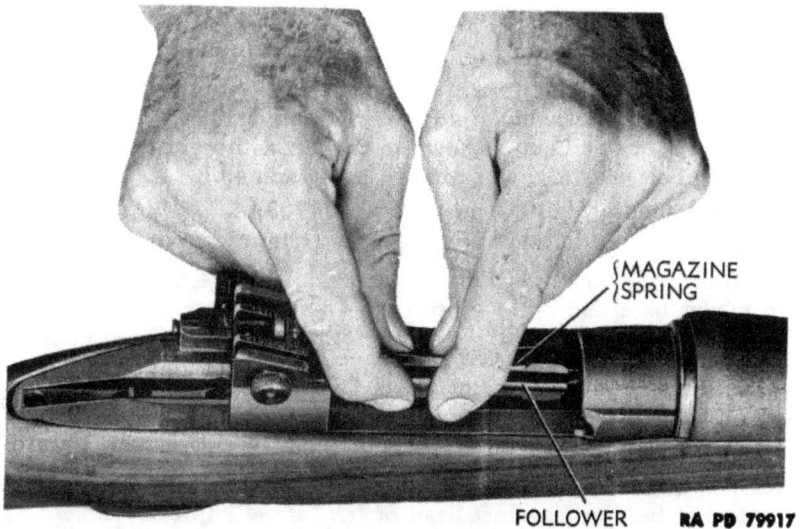

MAGAZINE SPRING

FOLLOWER   RA PD 79917

*Figure 39 — Inserting Assembled Magazine Spring and M1903A3
Type Follower in Rifle M1903A3*

type follower or the M1903A3 type follower as explained in paragraph
3 c (9) and 7 d. Method of reinstallation varies as explained below:

(1) M1903 TYPE FOLLOWER (fig. 37). With trigger guard magazine assembly removed, place assembled magazine spring and follower
in the magazine, spring first, and narrow end of follower forward.
Insert group into receiver from bottom and thread in guard screws
evenly and tightly (short screw forward). Depress follower on
spring a few times to assure proper seating.

(2) M1903A3 TYPE FOLLOWER (fig. 37). Reinstall magazine
spring and this type follower in the Rifle M1903A4 as explained in
step (1), above. If trigger guard magazine assembly has not been
removed, magazine spring and this type follower may be reinstalled
in the Rifle M1903A3 as follows:

(a) Position gun with muzzle to left.

(b) Insert small end of magazine spring under ears of follower and
slide fully forward.

(c) Compress magazine spring against follower and insert spring
and follower sidewise into magazine opening of receiver with small
end of follower toward the front and with spring toward *left* (near)
side of receiver (fig. 39).

(d) Rotate follower so that rib will project upward.

(e) Press rear end of follower down to bottom of magazine in
order to insure seating of spring under ears of follower.

c. **Bolt Group.** See that the cut-off is at center notch. Hold rifle
with fingers of left hand under receiver, and thumb extending over
left side of receiver. Take bolt in right hand, with safety lock in

41

ORDNANCE MAINTENANCE — U.S. RIFLES, CAL. .30, M1903, M1903A1, M1903A3 AND M1903A4

vertical position, safety lug up, and extractor alined with lower (unslotted) bolt locking lug. Press rear end of follower down with left thumb and push bolt into rear of receiver, lower bolt handle, turn safety lock and cut-off down to the left with right hand. When replacing bolt with new one, refer to paragraph 43 i.

d. Telescopic Sight Group, Rifle M1903A4.

(1) With *right* lateral adjusting screw removed from mount base, grasp sight just to rear of front mount ring. With sight at right angles to mount base and rear (eyepiece) end to right (bolt handle side) of receiver, insert mounting lug on front mount ring into mounting recess in front end of mount base.

(2) Press front mount ring down flat on base so that flat of ring lies on flat top of mount base.

(3) Swing rear (eyepiece) end of sight slowly to rear, towards receiver (fig. 34) until flat lug on rear mount ring is seated squarely on mount base and against head of *left* lateral adjusting screw. (It may be necessary to lift rear lug slightly to slide it on mount base. This usually indicates misalinement of mount rings which should be corrected (par. 58). *Do not force.*)

(4) Thread *right* lateral adjusting screw into mount base to hold rear mount ring in position. Be sure cupped heads of lateral adjusting screws are fully engaged in radial grooves of rear mount ring and mount base. If such engagement is difficult, it indicates that the flat lower faces of the lugs on mount rings are not parallel and the rings should be adjusted (par. 58).

NOTE: If mount rings become loose, or out of adjustment with respect to the mount base, they may be repositioned as explained in paragraph 58.

9. BOLT GROUP, DISASSEMBLY (figs. 42 and 43).

a. Hold bolt in left hand (fig. 40), press bolt sleeve lock in with thumb of right hand to unlock bolt sleeve from bolt, and unscrew bolt sleeve by turning to left. Firing pin should be cocked, and safety lock in the "SAFE" position.

b. Hold bolt sleeve between forefinger and thumb of left hand (fig. 41), draw cocking piece back with middle finger and thumb of right hand, and turn safety lock down to the "READY" position with the forefinger of the right hand. This allows the cocking piece to move forward in the bolt sleeve, thus partially relieving the tension of the mainspring. Care should be exercised in this operation to avoid pinching the fingers when the spring pressure is released.

c. With the cocking piece against the breast, draw back firing pin sleeve with forefinger and thumb of right hand and, holding it in this position, remove striker with the left hand. Remove firing pin sleeve

DISASSEMBLY AND ASSEMBLY

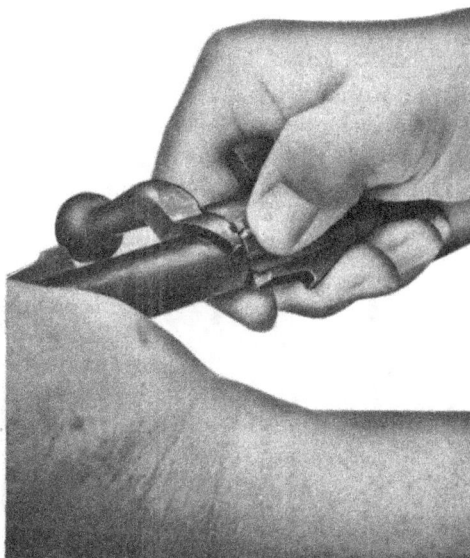

A. DEPRESSING BOLT SLEEVE LOCK   RA PD 7611

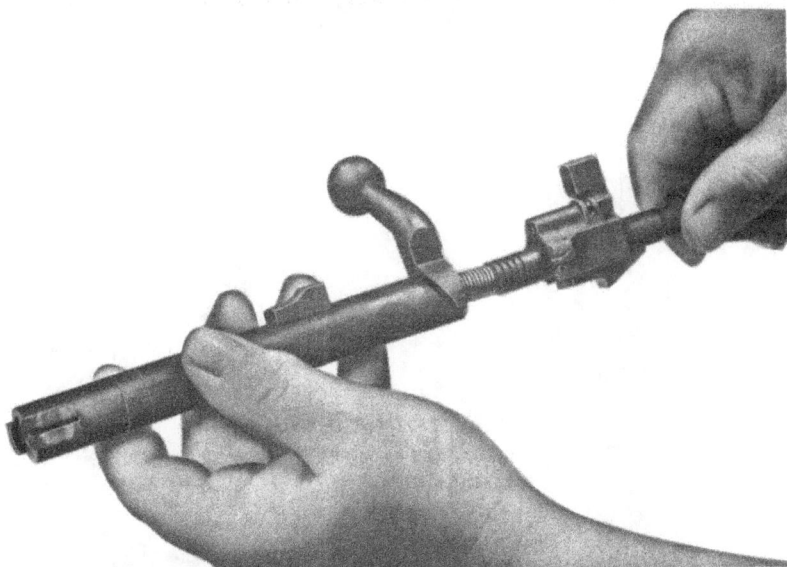

b. REMOVING FIRING PIN MECHANISM   RA PD 7612

Figure 40 — Disassembling Bolt Group

ORDNANCE MAINTENANCE — U.S. RIFLES, CAL. .30,
M1903, M1903A1, M1903A3 AND M1903A4

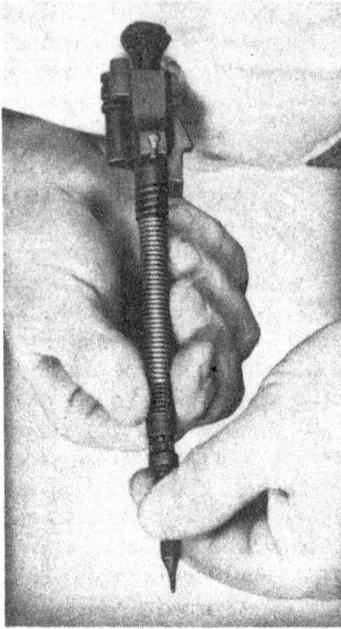

A. BEFORE TURNING SAFETY LOCK   RA PD 7613

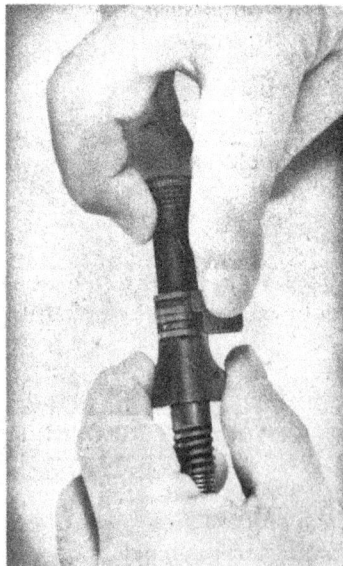

B. AFTER TURNING SAFETY LOCK   RA PD 7614

C. REMOVING STRIKER   RA PD 7615

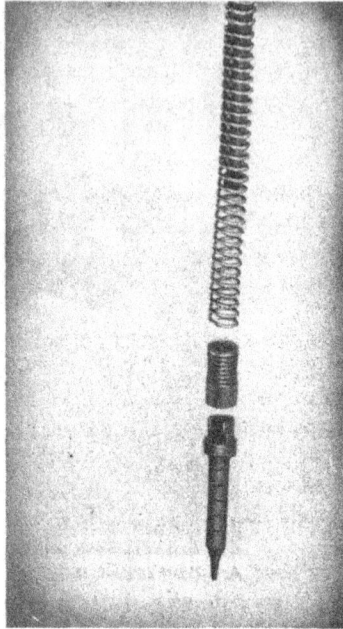

D. STRIKER AND SLEEVE REMOVED   RA PD 7616

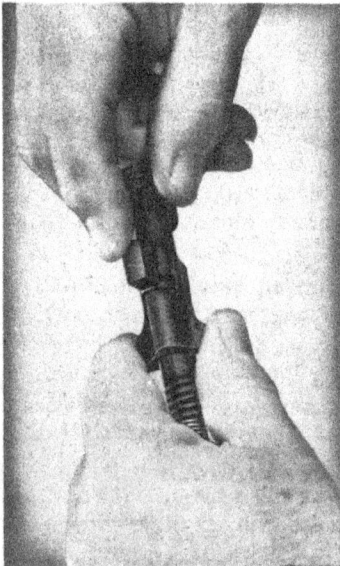

Figure 41 — Disassembling Bolt Group

and mainspring; pull firing pin out of bolt sleeve. In releasing pressure of mainspring, take care to point striker away from all personnel. Relieve pressure gradually to avoid losing parts.

d. Turn extractor to right, forcing its tongue out of its groove in the front of bolt. Force extractor forward and off bolt.

e. The extractor collar is bent into position on the bolt in manufacture and, together with the bolt, forms a permanent assembly known as the bolt assembly.

f. Turn safety lock to dismounting bevel position on the bolt sleeve halfway between the "READY" and the vertical position. Remove it by striking front face of thumb piece a light blow. The safety lock spindle is driven into the thumb piece and headed over at manufacture, forming a permanent assembly which includes the safety lock plunger and spring.

g. Drive out bolt sleeve lock pin from top, and remove bolt sleeve lock and spring, being careful not to lose spring.

h. The firing pin rod is screwed into the cocking piece and riveted at manufacture. Together, they form a permanent assembly called the firing pin assembly.

10. BOLT GROUP, ASSEMBLY (figs. 42 and 43).

a. In assembling the bolt sleeve lock to the bolt sleeve, be careful to compress the lock and spring while driving in the pin from the bottom of the bolt sleeve.

b. To assemble the safety lock and bolt sleeve, insert the safety lock spindle in its hole in the bolt sleeve as far as it will go. Then, with thumb piece vertical and pressed against some rigid object, introduce the point of the safety lock assembling tool provided for this purpose, or a small screwdriver, if the special tool is not available, between the safety-lock spindle and safety-lock plunger, forcing the latter into the thumb piece until it slips over the edge of the sleeve (fig. 44). Further pressure on the safety-lock thumb piece, together with the gradual withdrawal of the tool, will complete the assembling.

c. With the left hand, grasp rear of bolt, handle up, and turn extractor collar with thumb and forefinger of right hand until its lug is on a line with the safety lug on bolt. Take extractor in the right hand and insert lug on collar in undercuts in extractor by pushing extractor to rear until its tongue comes in contact with rim on face of bolt. A slight pressure with the left thumb on top of rear part of extractor assists in this operation. Turn extractor to right until it is over the right lug. Take bolt in right hand and press hook of extractor against butt plate or some rigid object until tongue on extractor enters its groove in bolt.

d. With safety lock turned down to the "READY" position to permit the firing pin to enter the bolt sleeve as far as possible, assemble

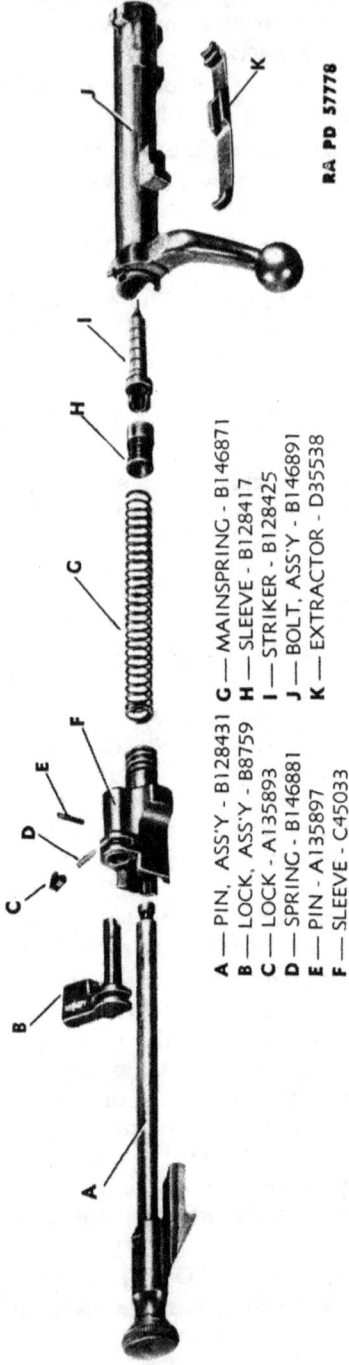

RA PD 57778

K

J

I

H

G

F

E

D

C

B

A

A — PIN, ASS'Y - B128431
B — LOCK, ASS'Y - B8759
C — LOCK - A135893
D — SPRING - B146881
E — PIN - A135897
F — SLEEVE - C45033

G — MAINSPRING - B146871
H — SLEEVE - B128417
I — STRIKER - B128425
J — BOLT, ASS'Y - B146891
K — EXTRACTOR - D35538

Figure 42 — Bolt Group — Exploded View — Parts for U.S. Rifles, cal. .30, M1903 and M1903A1

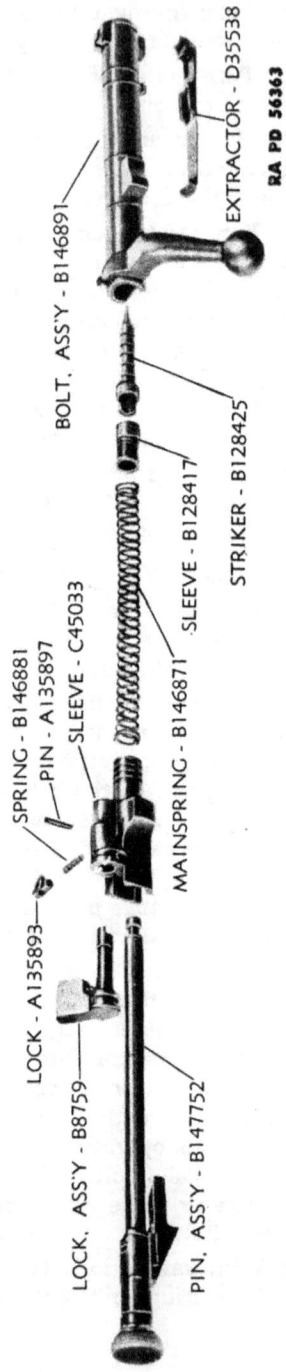

EXTRACTOR - D35538

RA PD 56363

BOLT. ASS'Y - B146891

STRIKER - B128425

SLEEVE - B128417

SPRING - B146881
PIN - A135897
SLEEVE - C45033

MAINSPRING - B146871

LOCK - A135893

LOCK. ASS'Y - B8759

PIN. ASS'Y - B147752

Figure 43 — Bolt Group — Exploded View — Parts for U. S. Rifles, cal. .30, M1903A3 (Bolt Assembly B147820 Is Used in This Group When Assembled to the Rifle M1903A4)

DISASSEMBLY AND ASSEMBLY

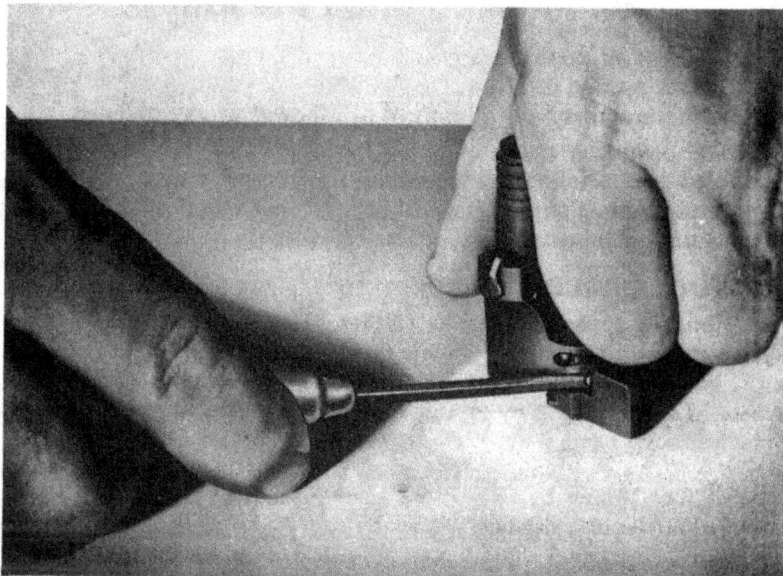

RA PD 39748

Figure 44 — Assembling Safety Lock to Bolt Sleeve,
Using Safety Lock Assembling Tool

bolt sleeve and firing pin. Place cocking piece against the breast and put on mainspring, firing pin sleeve, and striker. Hold cocking piece between thumb and forefinger of left hand, and by pressing the striker point against some substance not hard enough to injure it, force cocking piece back until the safety lock can be turned to the vertical position with right hand.

e. Insert firing pin in bolt and screw up bolt sleeve (by turning it to right) until bolt sleeve lock enters its notch on bolt.

11. FLOOR PLATE, MAGAZINE SPRING, AND FOLLOWER GROUP; DISASSEMBLY (figs. 47 and 49).

a. Raise rear end of lower portion of the magazine spring high enough to clear lug on floor plate and draw spring out of its mortise (Rifles M1903 and M1903A1). Proceed in the same manner to remove the follower.

b. The magazine spring of the Rifles M1903A3 and M1903A4 is disassembled from the follower in a similar manner. There is no floor plate in these rifles.

12. FLOOR PLATE, MAGAZINE SPRING, AND FOLLOWER GROUP; ASSEMBLY (figs. 47 and 49).

a. To assemble the magazine spring and follower to the floor plate (Rifles M1903 and M1903A1), insert larger end of magazine spring in the mortise of floor plate and push in as far as possible. (Rear end of lower portion must lie ahead of lug on rear end of floor plate.) Insert other end of spring in mortise of follower in like manner.

b. The magazine spring of the Rifles M1903A3 and M1903A4 is assembled to the follower by pushing the narrow end of the spring into the retaining slot in bottom of follower, and then pushing spring forward until retained by projection on rear end.

13. STOCK GROUP, DISASSEMBLY (figs. 48, 50, 51, and 53).

a. Remove upper band screw (Rifles M1903 and M1903A1) and drive upper band forward by a few short blows on the lug with a hard wood block. Unscrew stacking swivel screw and remove stacking swivel. (In order to remove upper band from barrel, it is necessary first to remove front sight movable stud (par. 15).)

NOTE: The bayonet stud band of the Rifles M1903A3 and M1903A4, which corresponds to the upper band of the Rifles M1903 and M1903A1, is removed in a similar manner by removing the bayonet stud band screw. The front sight group must be removed before the band can be removed from the barrel of the M1903A3. There is no front sight on the Rifle M1903A4. The stacking swivel band can then be removed by loosening the stacking swivel screw. The end of this screw is expanded and should not be removed from the band, else the threads will be stripped.

b. Unscrew lower band screw and remove lower band swivel (Rifles M1903 and M1903A1). Press in rear end of lower band spring and move lower band forward (fig. 46) beyond end of stock.

NOTE: End of lower band screw of Rifles M1903A3 and M1903A4 is expanded and should not be removed, else threads will be stripped. To remove band from stock, back out screw about ⅛ inch, spread prongs of band, depress lower band spring, and move band forward beyond end of stock.

c. Draw hand guard assembly (fig. 45) forward until free of fixed base (Rifles M1903 and M1903A1) and remove. Do not remove clips unless necessary, as they may become bent out of shape.

NOTE: Barrel guard assembly of Rifles M1903A3 and M1903A4 (fig. 53) is removed in a similar manner by drawing free of barrel guard ring. The barrel guard ring can be removed by sliding forward, if all other bands have been removed.

d. Remove front and rear guard screws and trigger guard group (fig. 47) (Rifles M1903 and M1903A1). It may be necessary to tap gently on front and rear of trigger guard to loosen. To remove floor plate catch and spring from trigger guard, drive out the floor plate catch pin from either side.

NOTE: Trigger guard magazine assembly of Rifles M1903A3

DISASSEMBLY AND ASSEMBLY

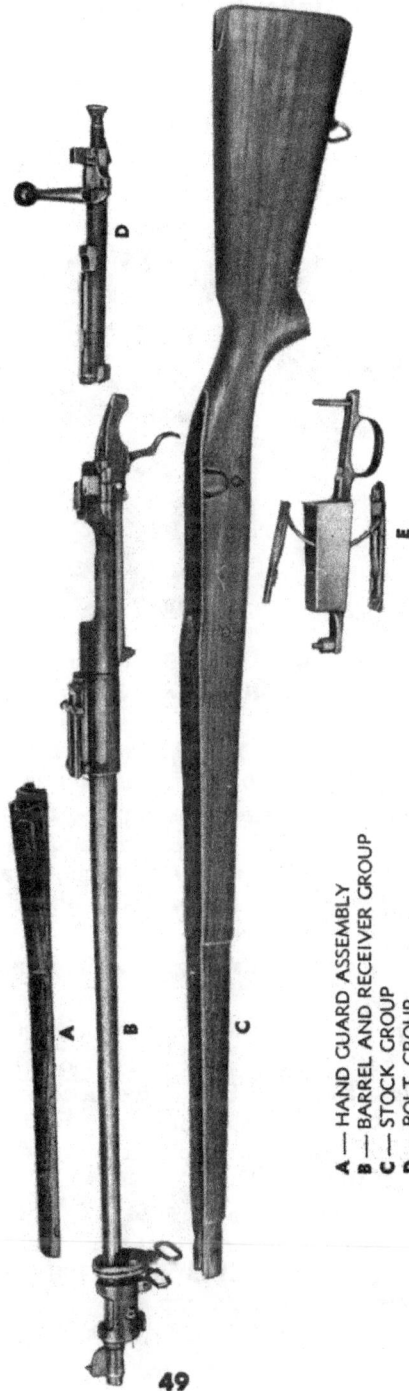

RA PD 84303

A — HAND GUARD ASSEMBLY
B — BARREL AND RECEIVER GROUP
C — STOCK GROUP
D — BOLT GROUP
E — TRIGGER GUARD GROUP

Figure 45 — Rifle Disassembled Into Groups — U.S. Rifle, cal. .30, M1903A1

**ORDNANCE MAINTENANCE — U.S. RIFLES, CAL. .30,
M1903, M1903A1, M1903A3 AND M1903A4**

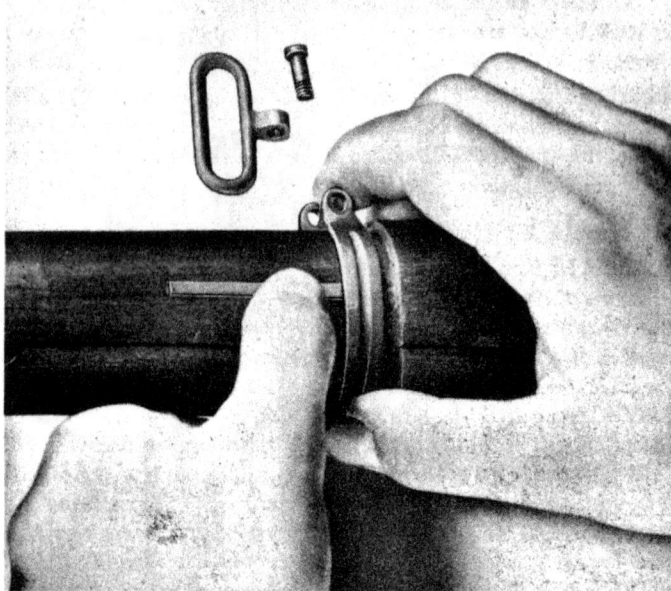

RA PD 7619
*Figure 46 — Depressing Lower Band Spring to Remove Lower
Band — Parts for U.S. Rifles, cal. .30, M1903 and M1903A1*

and M1903A4 is removed in a similar manner by removing guard
screws (fig. 49). There is no floor plate catch in this assembly.

e. Remove barrel and receiver assembly group from stock (fig. 45).
*The barrel is threaded into the receiver and assembled to it at the
time of manufacture, to be issued in that manner as a single assembly.
They should never be unscrewed except at an ordnance establishment
properly equipped for this work.*

f. To remove lower band spring, drive its spindle out of its hole in
stock from the left.

g. To remove guard screw bushing, punch out from top or bottom.

h. Unscrew butt swivel screws and remove butt swivel assembly
from stock (fig. 48). The butt swivel assembly, consisting of the
plate, swivel, and pin, is permanently assembled and issued complete.

NOTE: There is no pin in the butt swivel assembly of the Rifles
M1903A3 and M1903A4 (fig. 50).

i. To remove butt plate assembly (fig. 48), unscrew butt plate
screws. To disassemble, unscrew butt plate spring screw and remove
butt plate spring (Rifles M1903 and M1903A1). Drive out butt
plate pin and remove butt plate cap.

NOTE: Butt plate trap pin of Rifles M1903A3 and M1903A4

DISASSEMBLY AND ASSEMBLY

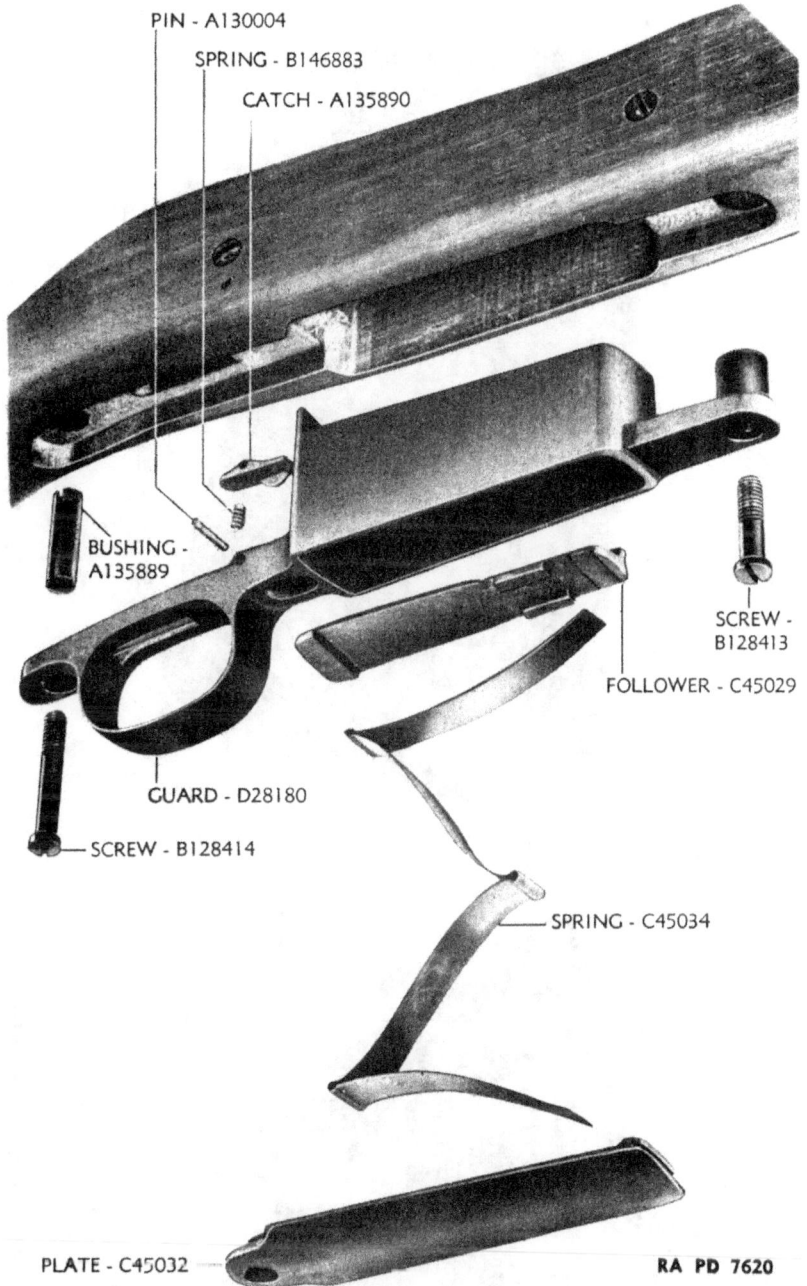

PIN - A130004

SPRING - B146883

CATCH - A135890

BUSHING - A135889

SCREW - B128413

FOLLOWER - C45029

GUARD - D28180

SCREW - B128414

SPRING - C45034

PLATE - C45032

RA PD 7620

*Figure 47 — Trigger Guard and Floor Plate Group — Exploded
View — Parts for U.S. Rifles, cal. .30, M1903 and M1903A1*

ORDNANCE MAINTENANCE — U.S. RIFLES, CAL. .30,
M1903, M1903A1, M1903A3 AND M1903A4

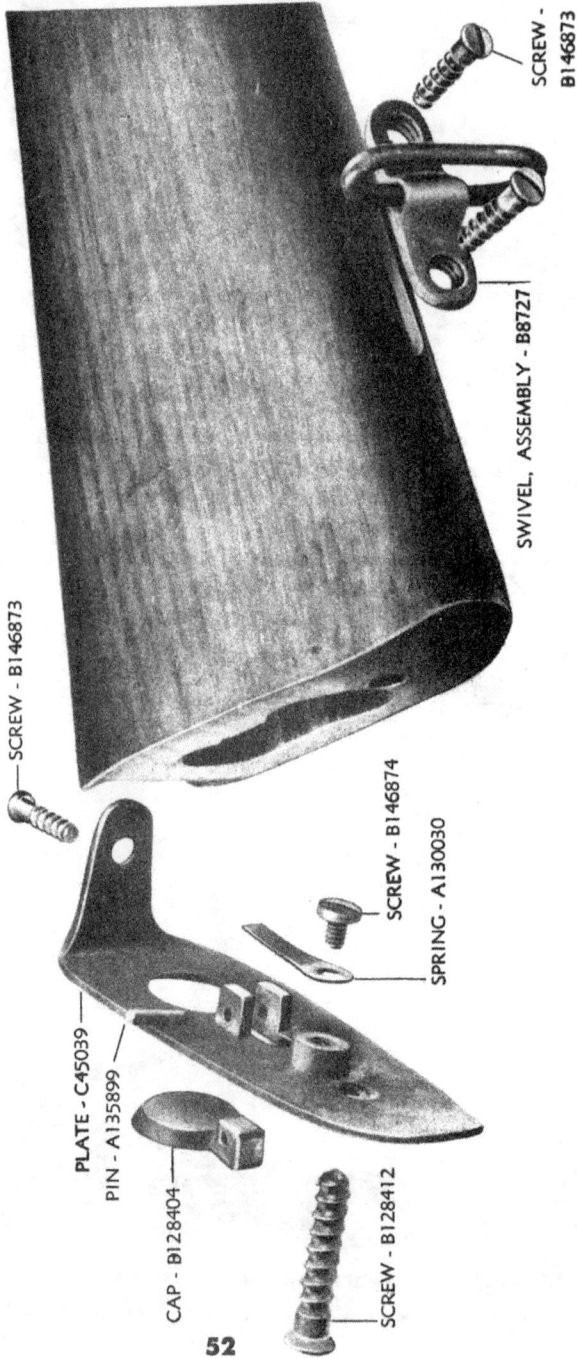

SCREW - B146873

RA PD 21974

SWIVEL, ASSEMBLY - B8727

SCREW - B146873

SCREW - B146874

SPRING - A130030

PLATE - C45039

PIN - A135899

CAP - B128404

SCREW - B128412

Figure 48 — Butt Plate and Butt Swivel Groups — Exploded View — Parts for U.S. Rifles, cal. .30, M1903 and M1903A1

52

DISASSEMBLY AND ASSEMBLY

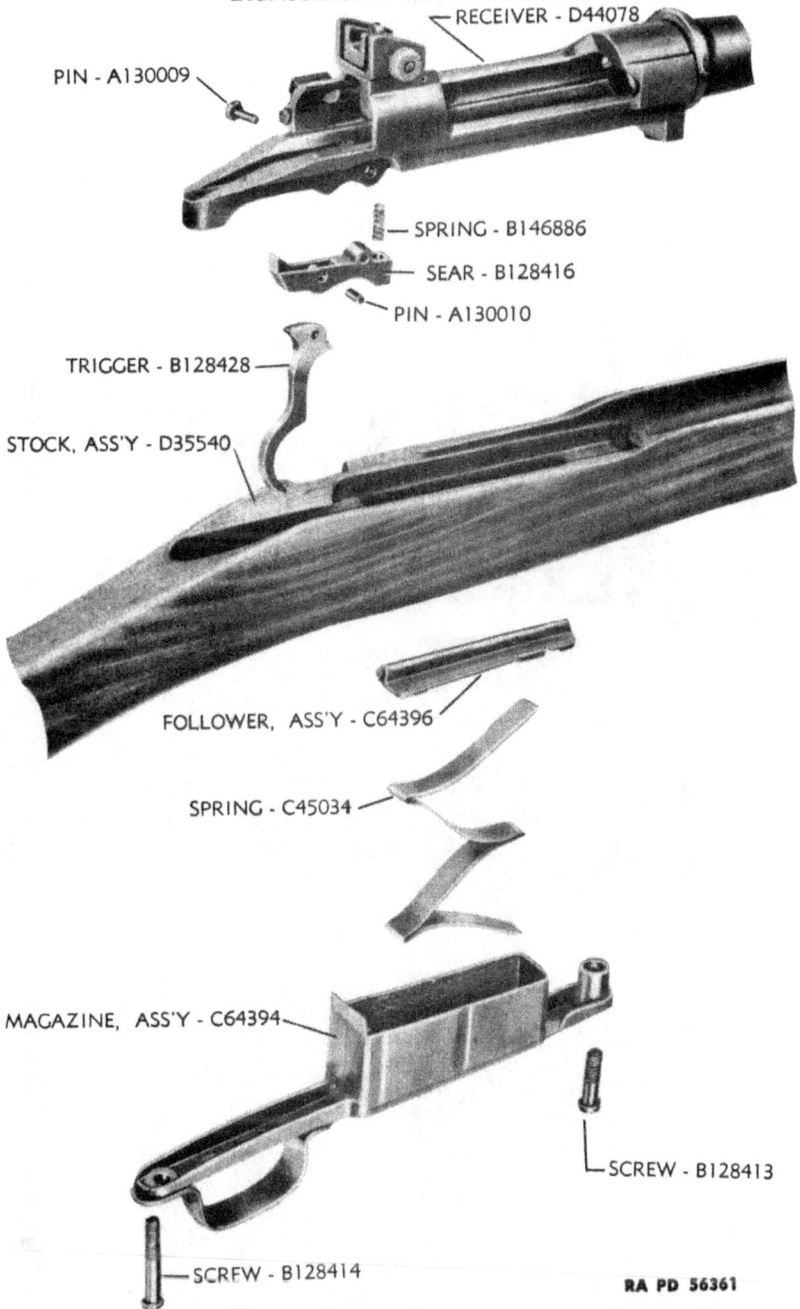

PIN - A130009

RECEIVER - D44078

SPRING - B146886

SEAR - B128416

PIN - A130010

TRIGGER - B128428

STOCK, ASS'Y - D35540

FOLLOWER, ASS'Y - C64396

SPRING - C45034

MAGAZINE, ASS'Y - C64394

SCREW - B128413

SCREW - B128414

RA PD 56361

*Figure 49 — Trigger Guard Magazine and Trigger Group —
Exploded View — Parts for U.S. Rifles, cal. .30,
M1903A3 and M1903A4*

ORDNANCE MAINTENANCE — U.S. RIFLES, CAL. .30,
M1903, M1903A1, M1903A3 AND M1903A4

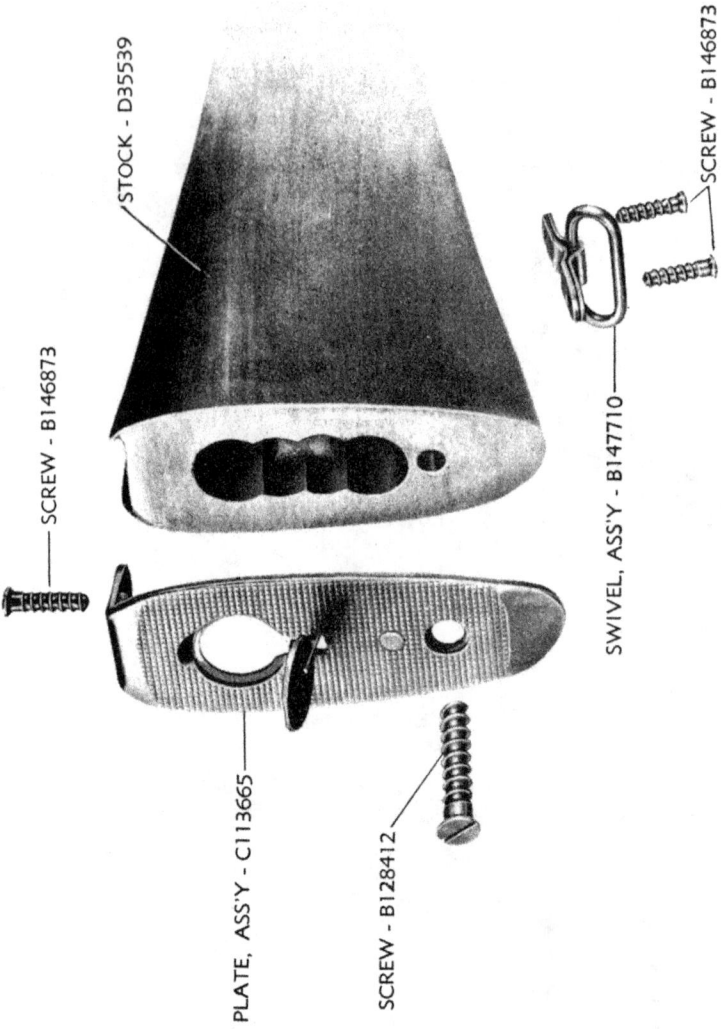

RA PD 56366

STOCK - D35539

SCREW - B146873

SCREW - B146873

SCREW - B146873

SWIVEL, ASS'Y - B147710

PLATE, ASS'Y - C113665

SCREW - B128412

*Figure 50 — Butt Plate and Butt Swivel Groups — Exploded View — Parts for U.S. Rifles,
cal. .30, M1903A3 and M1903A4*

DISASSEMBLY AND ASSEMBLY

(corresponding to butt plate pin Rifles M1903 and M1903A1) is upset at ends at manufacture and should not be removed.

j. The front and rear stock screws (or pins) serve merely to reinforce the stock, and should not be removed unless necessary for repair or replacements.

14. STOCK GROUP, ASSEMBLY (figs. 48, 50, 51, and 53).

a. Assemble butt plate cap and pin to butt plate. Place butt plate spring on shank of cap, curved side down, and thread in butt plate spring screw (M1903 and M1903A1 Rifles).

b. Place butt plate assembly on butt of stock and thread in butt plate screws. Short screw passes through top tang of butt plate.

c. Place butt swivel assembly in its seat in under side of stock butt, and thread in screws.

d. Insert and drive home guard screw bushing in its seat in under side of stock to rear of magazine opening.

e. Insert spindle of lower band spring in hole in right side of stock and drive in with wood block, so that spring seats in its groove in stock.

f. Reinstall barrel and receiver assembly group in stock.

g. Assemble floor plate catch spring and catch to trigger guard, and drive in catch pin. Insert trigger guard in stock and thread in front (short) and rear (long) guard screws (Rifles M1903 and M1903A1).

NOTE: There is no floor plate catch group in trigger guard magazine assembly of the Rifles M1903A3 and M1903A4. This assembly is assembled to the rifle in a similar manner.

h. For Rifles M1903 and M1903A1, place hand guard assembly on top of barrel, and slide upper and lower bands into place to bind stock and hand guard together. The lower band is stamped with the letter "U," which should face toward the muzzle when band is assembled. The band is tapered to fit hand guard and stock. Reassemble lower band swivel to lower band and stacking swivel to upper band, and thread in upper band screw from right side.

NOTE: In Rifles M1903A3 and M1903A4 the barrel guard and the bayonet stud band correspond to the hand guard and upper band of the Rifles M1903 and M1930A1. The stacking swivel band must be assembled to the stock and barrel guard before the bayonet stud band. (If removed, the barrel guard ring must be assembled to the barrel before the above parts are assembled.)

15. BARREL GROUP, DISASSEMBLY (figs. 51, 52, 53, and 54).

a. Remove front sight pin by driving out from left and remove front sight (fig. 51). Unscrew front sight screw and remove movable stud (Rifles M1903 and M1903A1), by tapping out laterally.

ORDNANCE MAINTENANCE — U.S. RIFLES, CAL. .30,
M1903, M1903A1, M1903A3 AND M1903A4

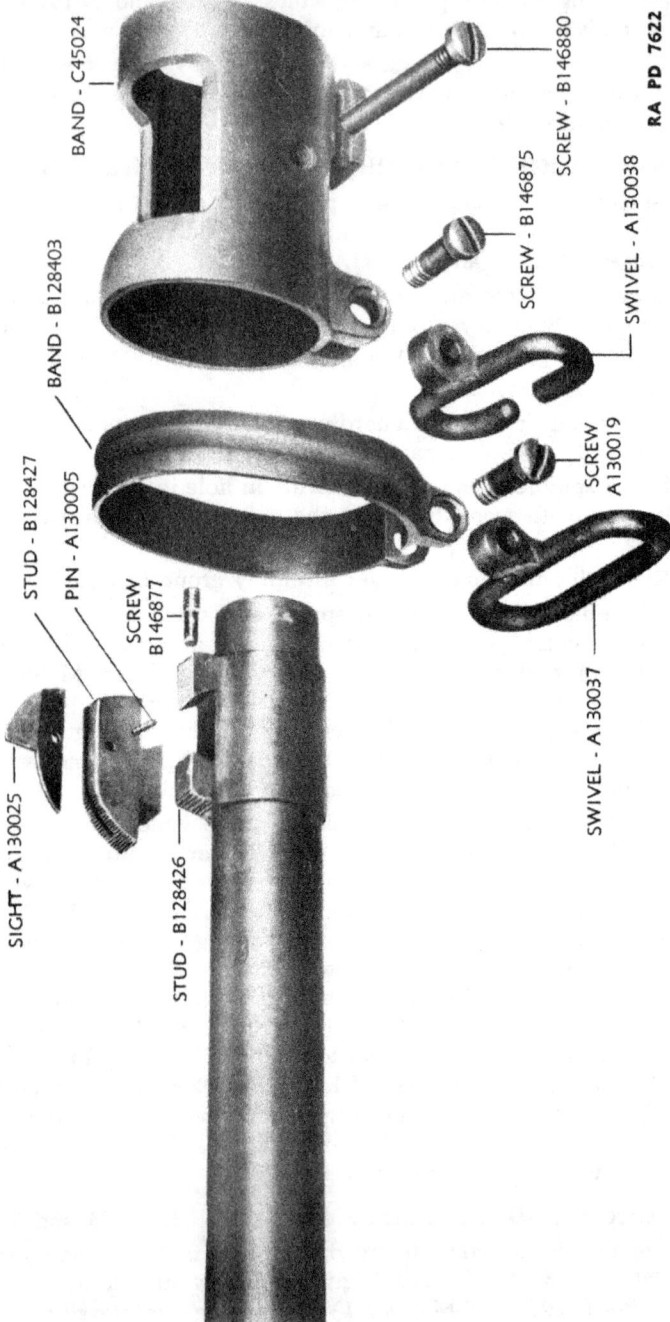

BAND - C45024

SCREW - B146880

RA PD 7622

SCREW - B146875

SWIVEL - A130038

BAND - B128403

SCREW
A130019

STUD - B128427

PIN - A130005

SCREW
B146877

SIGHT - A130025

SWIVEL - A130037

STUD - B128426

Figure 51 — Upper and Lower Bands and Front Sight Groups — Exploded View — Parts for
U.S. Rifles, cal. .30, M1903 and M1903A1

DISASSEMBLY AND ASSEMBLY

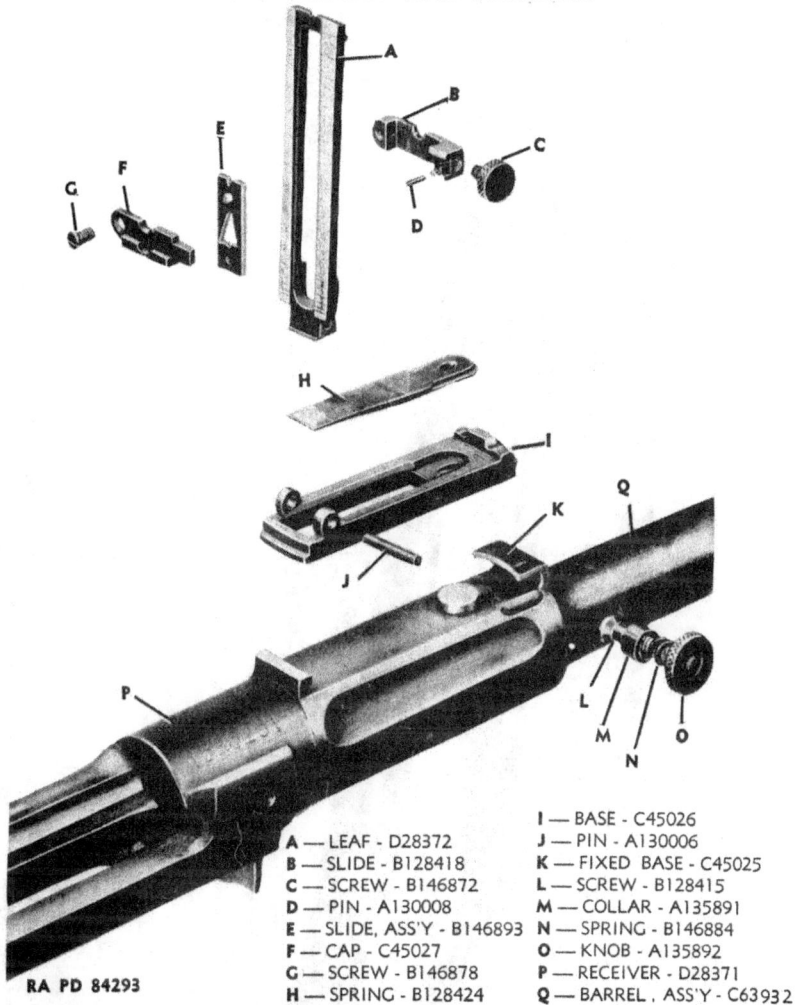

A — LEAF - D28372
B — SLIDE - B128418
C — SCREW - B146872
D — PIN - A130008
E — SLIDE, ASS'Y - B146893
F — CAP - C45027
G — SCREW - B146878
H — SPRING - B128424

I — BASE - C45026
J — PIN - A130006
K — FIXED BASE - C45025
L — SCREW - B128415
M — COLLAR - A135891
N — SPRING - B146884
O — KNOB - A135892
P — RECEIVER - D28371
Q — BARREL , ASS'Y - C63932

RA PD 84293

Figure 52 — Rear Sight Group — Exploded View — Parts for
U.S. Rifles, cal. .30, M1903 and M1903A1

b. The fixed stud should never be removed from the barrel unless necessary. To remove, drive out fixed stud pin and drive fixed stud forward by striking with a hard wood block.

NOTE: The front sight base of the Rifle M1903A3 (fig. 54) corresponds to the fixed stud of the Rifles M1903 and M1903A1, and is keyed to the barrel. It may be removed by removing the front sight base pin and driving forward off barrel as in subparagraph b, above. The key may then be lifted from slot in the barrel.

ORDNANCE MAINTENANCE — U.S. RIFLES, CAL. .30,
M1903, M1903A1, M1903A3 AND M1903A4

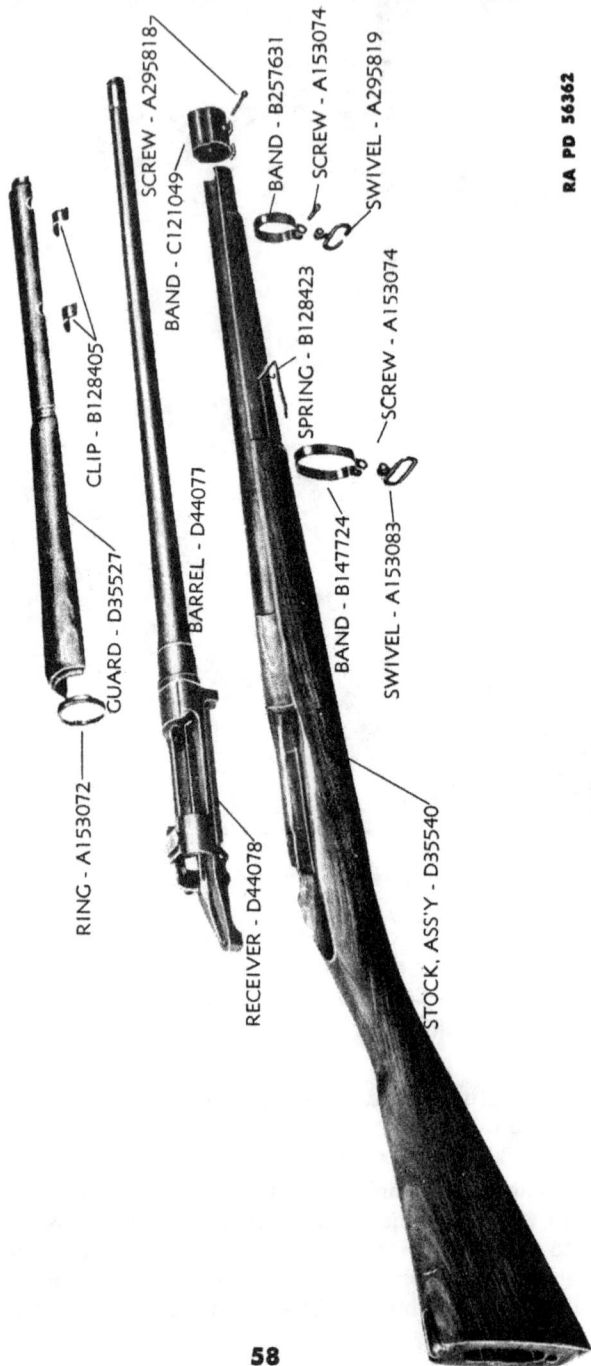

RA PD 56362

RING - A153072

GUARD - D35527

CLIP - B128405

SCREW - A295818

BAND - B257631

SCREW - A153074

SWIVEL - A295819

BAND - C121049

BARREL - D44077

SPRING - B128423

SCREW - A153074

RECEIVER - D44078

BAND - B147724

SWIVEL - A153083

STOCK, ASS'Y - D35540

Figure 53 — Stock, Barrel, and Receiver Group — Exploded View — (Front and Rear Sight and Butt Plate Groups Removed) — Parts for U.S. Rifle, cal. .30, M1903A3

DISASSEMBLY AND ASSEMBLY

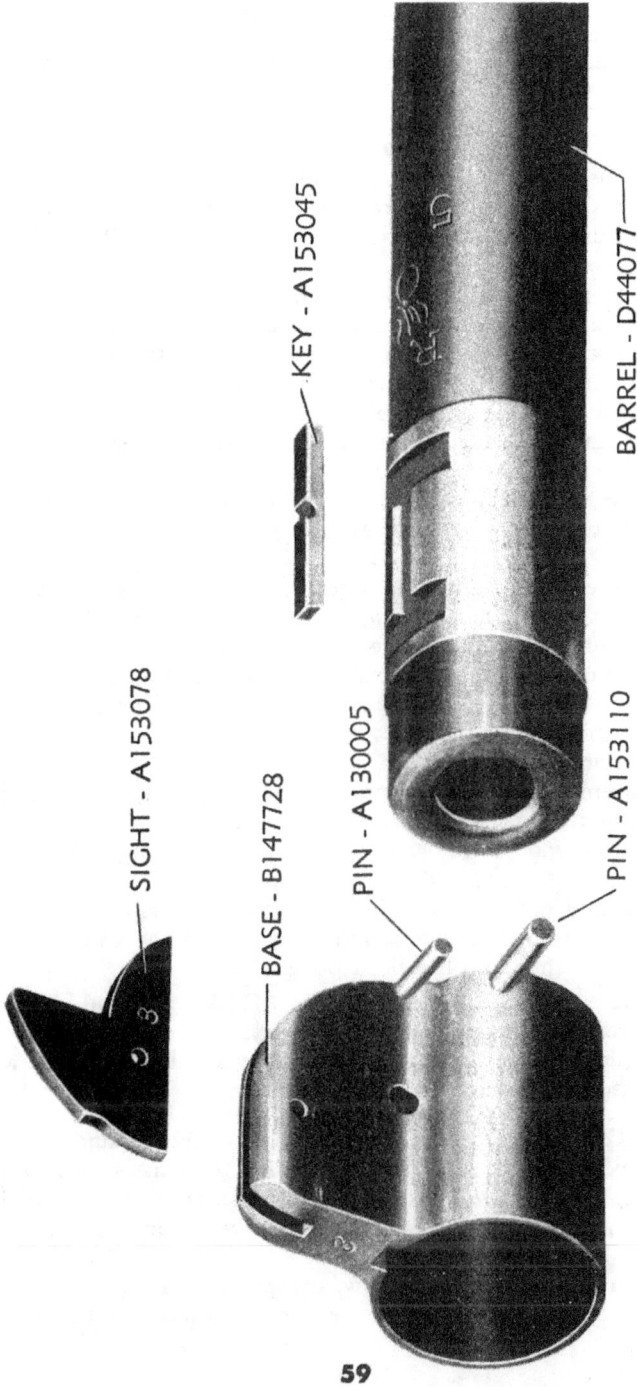

SIGHT - A153078

BASE - B147728

PIN - A130005

PIN - A153110

KEY - A153045

BARREL - D44077

RA PD 56364

Figure 54 — Front Sight Group — Exploded View — Parts for U.S. Rifle, cal. .30, M1903A3

ORDNANCE MAINTENANCE — U.S. RIFLES, CAL. .30,
M1903, M1903A1, M1903A3 AND M1903A4

c. To remove the rear sight assembly (Rifles M1903 and M1903A1) from the fixed base and to disassemble (fig. 52), proceed as follows:

(1) Turn windage screw until movable base has revolved far enough to disengage the worm gear on base lip from screw threads on windage screw, and the front and rear lips of movable base are not held by undercuts on the fixed base. Lift movable base off pivot lug on fixed base.

(2) Turn rear sight leaf to forward horizontal position. Place movable base in a vise with a small block of wood bearing on rear sight base spring as near to joint of sight leaf as possible (fig. 55). Be sure that no pressure of the vise is exerted on the ears or shoulder of movable base. Tighten vise gently so that block of wood will relieve pressure of spring on rear sight leaf and rear sight joint pin. Push or drive out pin using small pin drift, and remove rear sight leaf.

(3) Take movable base out of vise and drive sight base spring forward out of mortise in base, using a pin drift inserted in hole in spring.

(4) Unscrew rear sight slide cap screw from rear sight slide cap and drive out rear sight slide cap pin. Unscrew and take out rear sight slide binding screw. Drive rear sight slide cap very gently to left out of mortise in rear sight slide. Remove slide and cap from sight leaf and slide rear sight drift slide to top of leaf and out of groove in leaf. The drift slide pin is riveted in place at manufacture and is not to be removed.

(5) To remove rear sight windage screw from its position in fixed base, compress windage screw spring by forcing screw collar toward windage screw knob to allow as much play as possible, and tap alternately the taper head and the screw knob toward the breech until assembly comes out of seat. The windage screw assembly is made a permanent assembly at manufacture by having the end of the pin spun over after the knob has been put on.

d. The fixed base (Rifles M1903 and M1903A1) should never be removed from the barrel unless necessary. To remove, drive out fixed base pin and drive fixed base forward by striking with hard wood block, taking care not to damage overhanging lugs. Remove spline.

16. BARREL GROUP, ASSEMBLY (figs. 51, 52, 53, and 54).

a. If fixed base (Rifles M1903 and M1903A1) has been removed, assemble spline to barrel and drive fixed base on with block of hard wood until pin can be inserted in hole. Drive pin into hole securely. Then assemble rear sight as follows:

(1) To reinstall windage screw, compress windage screw spring as much as possible and slide windage screw into its position in fixed base.

DISASSEMBLY AND ASSEMBLY

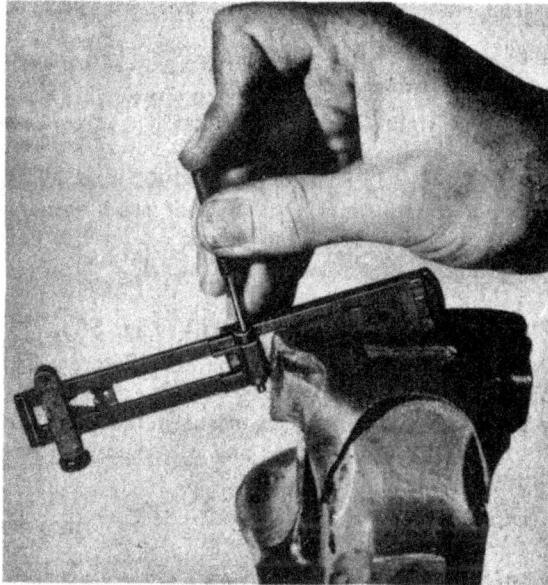

RA PD 16923

*Figure 55 — Removing Rear Sight Leaf Joint Pin —
Parts for U.S. Rifles, cal. .30, M1903 and M1903A1*

(2) Insert drift slide in sight leaf and assemble rear sight slide and cap. Care must be taken to insure that drift slide pin is in groove in slide cap before assembling cap and slide. Be sure to screw in rear sight slide binding screw before inserting slide cap pin. Screw in slide cap screw.

(3) Drive sight base spring into mortise in movable base, and place assembly in vise with block of wood in position as in disassembly (fig. 55). Compress spring just enough to allow sight leaf to be positioned and joint pin inserted. Take assembly out of vise and turn leaf down on movable base.

(4) Place movable base on pivot lug on fixed base and rotate to engage windage screw. In reengaging worm gear on movable base with threads on windage screw, allow them to engage by exerting only a gentle pressure, as undue force may damage threads.

b. If the fixed stud (front sight, M1903 and M1903A1 Rifles) has been removed, drive it on the barrel over spline, until fixed stud pin can be inserted in hole. Be sure pin and stud are secure.

NOTE: The front sight base of the Rifle M1903A3 is assembled in a similar manner. The front sight base key must first be seated (pin groove up) in its groove in the muzzle end of the barrel before driving the sight base on. There must be no movement of key when seated. If loose, peen in position (par. 46 c).

c. Assemble movable stud to fixed stud (M1903 and M1903A1 Rifles) and thread in front sight screw.

d. Assemble front sight (curved edge forward) and drive in front sight pin securely.

NOTE: The front band of the Rifles M1903 and M1903A1, and the stacking swivel band assembly, bayonet stud band, and barrel guard less ring, Rifle 1903A3, must be placed on the barrel before the front sight group is assembled to the barrel.

17. RECEIVER GROUP, DISASSEMBLY (fig. 56).

a. Remove the cut-off by loosening the cut-off screw in the end of the thumb piece until it disengages the groove in the cut-off spindle; insert the blade of a screwdriver in the notch in the rear of the spindle and force it out. Remove the spring and pluunger and cut-off screw. Be careful not to lose the spring and plunger.

b. Remove the ejector by driving out the ejector pin from the upper side.

c. Remove the sear, sear spring, and trigger by driving out the sear pin from the right.

d. Remove the trigger from the sear by driving out the trigger pin from either side.

e. Remove bolt stop assembly by inserting a small punch in the hole in the end of the spring and drawing it from its pocket until pin is free to be pulled out. The bolt stop pin and spring are a permanent assembly.

NOTE: Some Rifles M1903 and M1903A1 are without the bolt stop assembly (par. 43 i).

f. *To remove the rear sight assembly from the Rifle M1903A3 (fig. 57),* proceed as follows:

(1) Turn out the windage index knob screw located in the knurled edge of the knob, far enough to free the knob from the windage yoke screw, and pull knob from yoke screw. (Tighten windage index knob screw to prevent loss.)

(2) Turn out windage yoke screw from sight base, at same time holding remaining parts from springing out.

(3) Lift windage yoke and aperture group out of base, with care not to loose windage yoke plunger and spring located in bottom of yoke, and index knob spring located in right side of sight base. These parts can be pulled out.

(4) Loosen the aperture slide screw and pull slide aperture, with screw and slide aperture spring attached, forward out of windage yoke. Spring and screw can be removed from aperture if necessary.

(5) The sight base should not be removed unless necessary. To

DISASSEMBLY AND ASSEMBLY

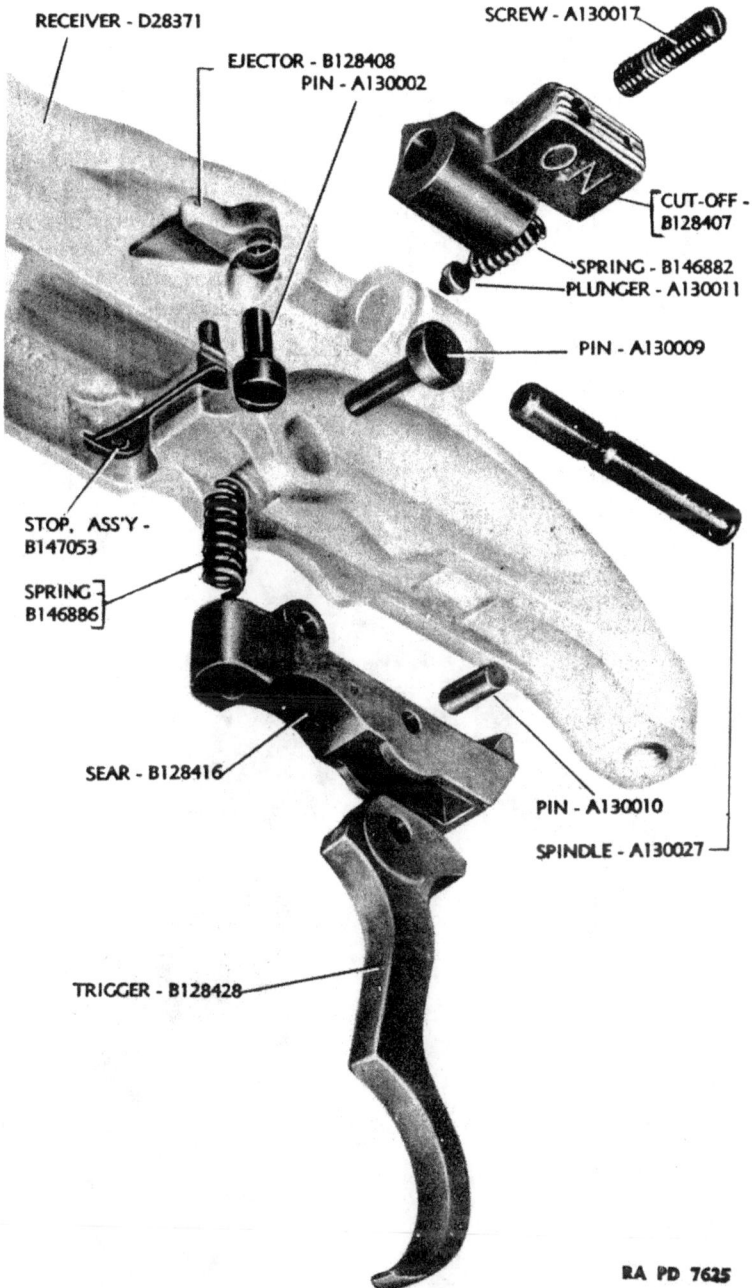

RECEIVER - D28371

SCREW - A130017

EJECTOR - B128408
PIN - A130002

CUT-OFF -
B128407

SPRING - B146882

PLUNGER - A130011

PIN - A130009

STOP, ASS'Y -
B147053

SPRING
B146886

SEAR - B128416

PIN - A130010

SPINDLE - A130027

TRIGGER - B128428

RA PD 7625

Figure 56 — Receiver Group — Exploded and Phantom View

ORDNANCE MAINTENANCE — U.S. RIFLES, CAL. .30,
M1903, M1903A1, M1903A3 AND M1903A4

RA PD 56365

A — SCREW - A153077
B — KNOB - A153069
C — SCREW - A153076
D — SPRING - A153080
E — YOKE - C113664
F — APERTURE - C113659
G — SPRING - A153082
H — SPRING - A153081
I — SCREW - A153075
J — PLUNGER - A153071
K — BASE - C113661
L — SCREW - B147726
M — EJECTOR - B128408
N — SPINDLE - A130027
O — PLUNGER - A130011
P — SPRING - B146882
Q — CUT-OFF - B128407
R — SCREW - A130017
S — PIN - A130002
T — RECEIVER - D44078

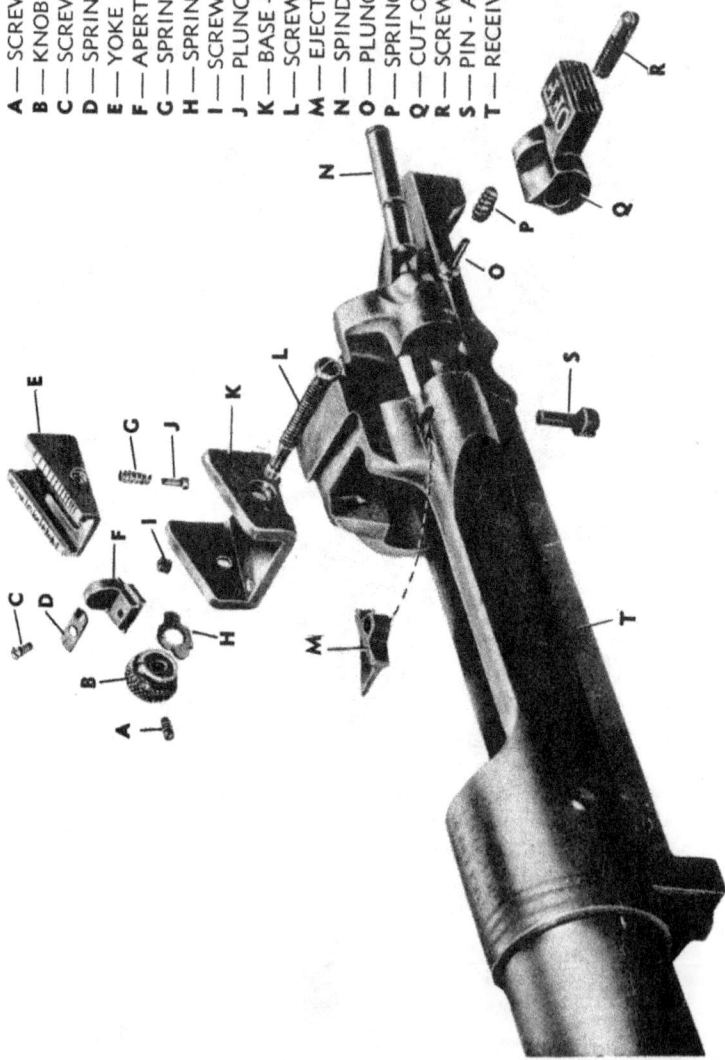

Figure 57 — Rear Sight and Cut-off Group — Exploded View — Parts for U.S. Rifle, cal. .30, M1903A3

64

remove, turn out base screw located in top of base, and drive base from receiver, using brass drift or hard wood block.

NOTE: Rear sight base screw A153075 has been eliminated in sights of recent manufacture. The sight base is now staked in place.

g. *To remove the (telescopic sight) mount base from the receiver of the Rifle M1903A4 (fig. 58),* proceed as follows:

(1) Using a small punch or screwdriver, drive back the staking of front and rear mount base screws sufficiently to clear slot in head of the screws.

(2) Turn out screws and lift base from receiver together with mount base shim which may be positioned under front or rear end of mount base. (The shim is used for leveling the base with respect to the bore line of the barrel when assembled at manufacture. It is provided in four thicknesses ranging from 0.005 to 0.020 inch. Its position and thickness should be noted as a guide when assembling. See paragraph 57 for explanation.)

18. RECEIVER GROUP, ASSEMBLY (fig. 56).

a. Assemble bolt stop assembly by inserting pin and seat spring in its pocket in receiver (to rear of magazine opening).

NOTE: Some Rifles M1903 and M1903A1 are without the bolt stop assembly (par. 43 i).

b. Position trigger and sear and insert trigger pin.

c. Place sear spring in position and compress it by pressing on sear until sear pin is inserted in hole.

d. Place the ejector in position and drive in the ejector pin.

e. Place the spring and plunger in position in the cut-off. Hold cut-off firmly in position while inserting the spindle, as spring and plunger may fly out when spring is compressed. Thread in cut-off screw, making sure that it is screwed in far enough to engage the spindle.

f. *To assemble the rear sight group of the Rifle M1903A3 (fig. 57),* proceed as follows:

(1) If sight has been removed, slide it onto dovetailed lug on bridge of receiver, with ears sloping up to rear. Qualify alinement mark on rear of base with that on bridge of receiver and thread in base screw tightly (NOTE, par. 17 f (5)).

(2) Place slide aperture spring on top of slide aperture with *wide* dimension (between screw hole and edge of spring) toward peephole in aperture and long end of spring to *left* so that protrusion will mate with retaining notches in left side of windage yoke. Insert aperture slide screw and turn in part way. Then insert the slide aperture, so assembled, into the guideways in low end of windage yoke with peep hole end leading. Tighten aperture slide screw.

ORDNANCE MAINTENANCE — U.S. RIFLES, CAL. .30,
M1903, M1903A1, M1903A3 AND M1903A4

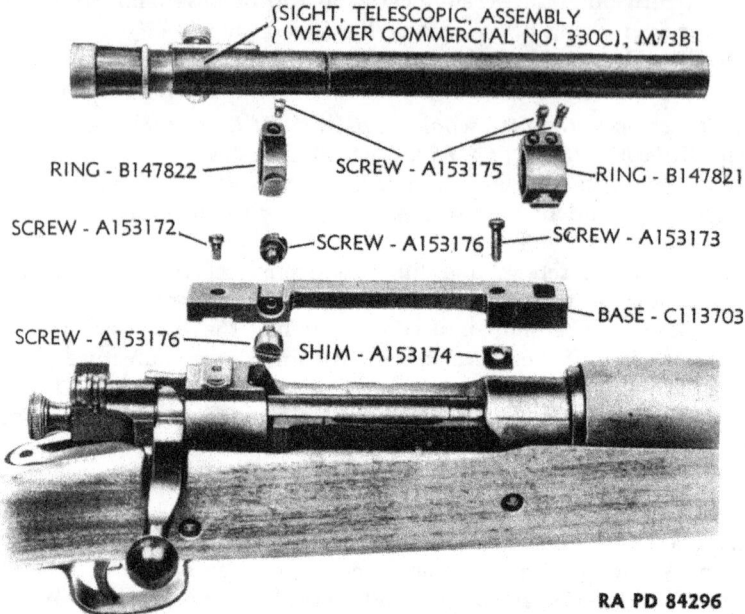

Figure 58 — Mount Base and Telescopic Sight M73B1 Group —
Exploded View — Parts for U.S. Rifle, cal. .30, M1903A4

(3) Insert windage yoke plunger and spring (spring first) into seat in bottom of windage yoke. Place assembled yoke between ears of sight base with ears of yoke facing same direction (rear) as those on base. Press down yoke against plunger spring, aline screw hole in yoke and base, and insert windage yoke screw from *left* side, through base and yoke, and thread all the way through.

(4) Place windage index knob spring over grooved end of windage yoke screw, and seating in counterbored recess in right side of sight base, with flat edge down, and bow facing out.

(5) Place windage index knob on grooved end of windage yoke screw, press in against spring, and turn in index knob (set) screw tightly. Be sure end of knob (set) screw seats in groove in yoke screw before tightening. There should be slight lateral movement of windage yoke screw when index knob is pressed to left against spring action of index knob spring, and then released.

(6) Test lateral movement of windage yoke by turning index knob, and test movement of slide aperture by sliding it up and down windage yoke ramp. The windage yoke should move freely the full width of the base, and the slide aperture should move the full length of the yoke ramp and be retained positively and without shake at the graduation notches. If this is not so, it is likely that the slide aperture spring is improperly assembled.

DISASSEMBLY AND ASSEMBLY

g. To assemble the (telescopic sight) mount base to the receiver of the Rifle M1903A4 (fig. 58), proceed as follows:

(1) Place mount base shim on top of front (or rear) end of the receiver as when disassembled, so that hole in shim registers with screw hole in receiver, and shim does not overhang receiver.

NOTE: The mount base of each Rifle M1903A4 is assembled, alined, and leveled at manufacture, and the screws staked in position; therefore, the same shim or one of like thickness (par. 57 a) must be used and placed in the same position when reassembling the base to the rifle in question (par. 57). For assembling a new mount base, refer to paragraph 57.

(2) Place mount base on receiver over shim, with curved end forward, and slotted rear end over lug on top of receiver bridge so that screw holes aline.

(3) Insert (long) front mount base screw through front end of base and shim (if shim is assembled in front) and thread into receiver.

(4) Insert (short) rear mount base screw through base and shim (if shim is assembled in rear) and thread into receiver.

(5) Turn both screws down evenly and tight, and stake securely in position.

(6) Set cross hairs of telescopic sight at zero windage and 100 yards elevation (point blank setting) as explained in TM 9-270, mount sight to base, and bore sight the rifle to check alinement of base as explained in paragraph 54.

19. BAYONET M1905, DISASSEMBLY (fig. 59).

a. Unscrew grip screw from right side of blade handle and lift off right and left grips with escutcheons assembled.

b. Press in on scabbard catch and pull bayonet catch slightly away from handle and to rear out of scabbard catch.

c. Pull scabbard catch and spring down out of well in handle.

d. Do not remove escutcheons from grips unless necessary as they will become loose in grips if disturbed. The guard is riveted to the blade at manufacture and should not be removed. If necessary to remove, drive out rivets. (Grips may be of composition with escutcheons sealed in.)

20. BAYONET M1905, ASSEMBLY (fig. 59).

a. Insert scabbard catch spring in well in blade handle just to rear of guard.

b. Insert small end of scabbard catch into well to bear on spring, with hook of catch projecting forward through slot in guard.

c. Press scabbard catch against spring and insert small end of bayonet catch, from left, through hole in scabbard catch. Push bayo-

ORDNANCE MAINTENANCE — U.S. RIFLES, CAL. .30, M1903, M1903A1, M1903A3 AND M1903A4

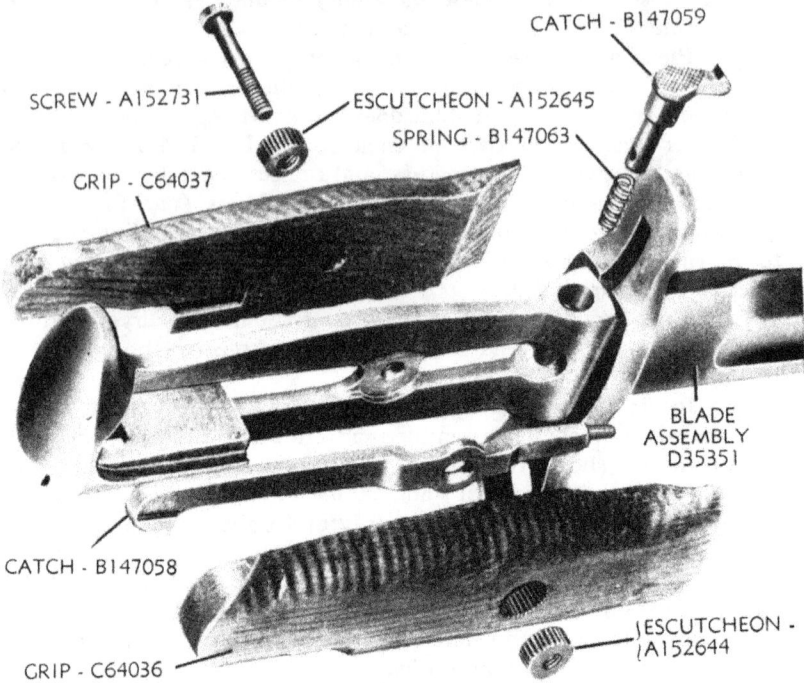

CATCH - B147059

SCREW - A152731

ESCUTCHEON - A152645

SPRING - B147063

GRIP - C64037

BLADE ASSEMBLY D35351

CATCH - B147058

ESCUTCHEON - A152644

GRIP - C64036

RA PD 84294

Figure 59 — Bayonet M1905 — Exploded View of Handle

net catch forward and in toward blade handle so that hook projects into bayonet stud slot in rear end of blade handle, and body of catch seats in cut in bridge of blade handle.

d. Reposition escutcheons in grips, if removed, and seat right grip on blade handle and insert grip screw through grip, blade handle, and bayonet catch. Then seat left grip, thread screw into it, and draw down tight.

e. Test both catches by pressing in scabbard catch and releasing. It should return by spring pressure and both catches should then be in locked position.

21. BAYONET M1, DISASSEMBLY (fig. 60).

a. This bayonet is basically identical with the Bayonet M1905 except for length of blade and minor points in design. The grips are of composition instead of wood. The escutcheons are sealed in at manufacture and should not be removed. Disassemble as prescribed for the Bayonet M1905 in paragraph 19.

DISASSEMBLY AND ASSEMBLY

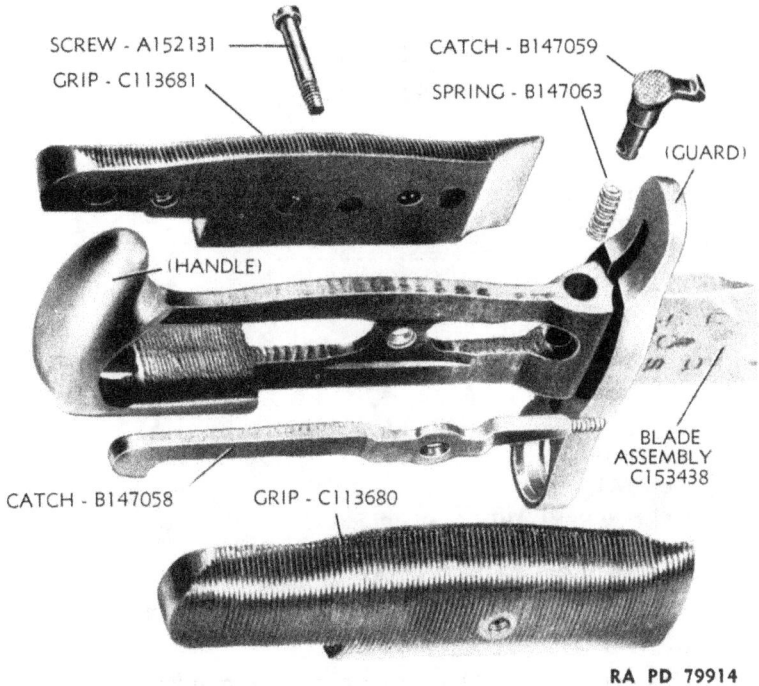

SCREW - A152131

GRIP - C113681

CATCH - B147059

SPRING - B147063

(GUARD)

(HANDLE)

CATCH - B147058

GRIP - C113680

BLADE
ASSEMBLY
C153438

RA PD 79914

Figure 60 — Bayonet M1 — Exploded View of Handle

22. BAYONET M1, ASSEMBLY (fig. 60).

a. This bayonet is basically identical with the Bayonet M1905 as stated in paragraph 21. Assemble as prescribed for the Bayonet M1905 in paragraph 20.

23. TELESCOPIC SIGHT (RIFLE M1903A4), DISASSEMBLY (figs. 8 and 58).

a. The telescopic sight used with the Rifle M1903A4 should not be disassembled. Removal of the mount rings is explained in paragraph 58. Damaged sights should be sent to a base shop (or the factory) for repair or disposal.

24. TELESCOPIC SIGHT (RIFLE M1903A4), ASSEMBLY (figs. 8 and 58).

a. There being no disassembly permitted of the telescopic sight used with the Rifle M1903A4 with the exception of the removal of the mount rings, no assembly is required except the replacement and adjustment of the mount rings when necessary. This procedure is explained in paragraph 58.

ORDNANCE MAINTENANCE — U.S. RIFLES, CAL. .30,
M1903, M1903A1, M1903A3 AND M1903A4

Section III
INSPECTION

25. GENERAL.

a. Inspection is for the purpose of determining the condition of the materiel and whether repairs or adjustments are required to insure serviceability.

b. Before inspection is begun, the materiel should be thoroughly cleaned to remove any fouling, dirt, or other foreign matter which might interfere with its proper functioning. For instructions in care and cleaning and the materials used, refer to FM 23-10, TM 9-850, SNL K-1, and paragraphs 59 and 60 of this manual.

26. INSPECTION REPORT.

a. The procedure to be followed relating to inspection is contained in TM-9 1100.

27. TOOLS FOR INSPECTION.

a. General Tools. General tools used for inspection are listed in SNL B-3 as company accessories for the rifle. They are also listed and shown in SNL B-20 and are carried on the small arms repair truck. These tools require no explanation of their use.

b. Special Tools. Special tools and gages used for inspection are listed and shown in SNL B-20 and are carried on the small arms repair truck. A general description of each tool is given below. For details of their use, see paragraph 28.

(1) BOLT, FIELD TEST, D1892. The field test bolt is used in

INSPECTION

conjunction with the headspace gages listed below to determine whether the chamber, bolt, lug seats in the receiver, or all three, are worn beyond serviceability. It is a gage made in the form of a rifle bolt without extractor or firing pin mechanism.

(2) GAGES, HEADSPACE, 1.940-INCH, C7719A; 1.946-INCH, C7719G; 1.950-INCH, C7719M. These gages are used with or without the field test bolt to determine headspace. The 1.950-inch gage is used for testing in the field, and the 1.940- and 1.946-inch gages are used for testing at an arsenal or depot. They are cylindrical in form and are inserted in the chamber similarly to a cartridge.

(3) GAGE, BREECH BORE, C3940. The breech bore gage is used to determine wear of the bore at the origin of rifling. The gage has a scale graduated to read in thousandths of an inch. It has the form of a tapered rod and is inserted in the bore at the breech. There are two types of breech bore gage with drawing number C3940. One gage has eight spaces between the rejection line for machine gun barrels and the rejection line for rifle barrels. The other type has nine spaces between these two rejection lines. See paragraph 28 d (2) for use of each type of bore gage.

(4) REFLECTOR, BARREL, CAL. .30, B147001. The barrel reflector is used for visual inspection of the bore and chamber of the rifle. It consists of a mirror mounted in a frame in such a manner that, when inserted in the chamber, the mirror affords a view of the rifle bore.

(5) WEIGHTS, TRIGGER PULL, AND HOOK. The weights are used to ascertain if the trigger pull lies between the limits of 3 and 6 pounds. They, and the hook for attaching them to the trigger, may be improvised locally or obtained from the small arms repair truck. (Note, par. 28 c (3)).

28. RIFLE AS A UNIT.

a. General. Inspect the rifle for general appearance, the metal parts for scratches, shiny spots, rust, and wear, and the wooden parts for condition and mutilation. Inspect heads of screws for burs. Check float of barrel (par. 45 a) and functioning of magazine spring and follower. Test complete action of rifle mechanism with clip of dummy cartridges.

b. Headspace. Headspace is determined by use of the headspace gages and field test bolt. The points of wear determined by these gages are shown in figure 61.

(1) In conducting field inspections of the rifle, headspace will be tested with the 1.950-inch headspace gage used in conjunction with the field test bolt. To make this test, proceed as follows: Insert the gage in the chamber and try closing the bolt on the gage. It should not close. CAUTION: *In making the test for headspace, the bolt handle should never be forced, but rather should be "felt" by using only the thumb, first and second fingers of the right hand on the ball of the*

ORDNANCE MAINTENANCE — U.S. RIFLES, CAL. .30,
M1903, M1903A1, M1903A3 AND M1903A4

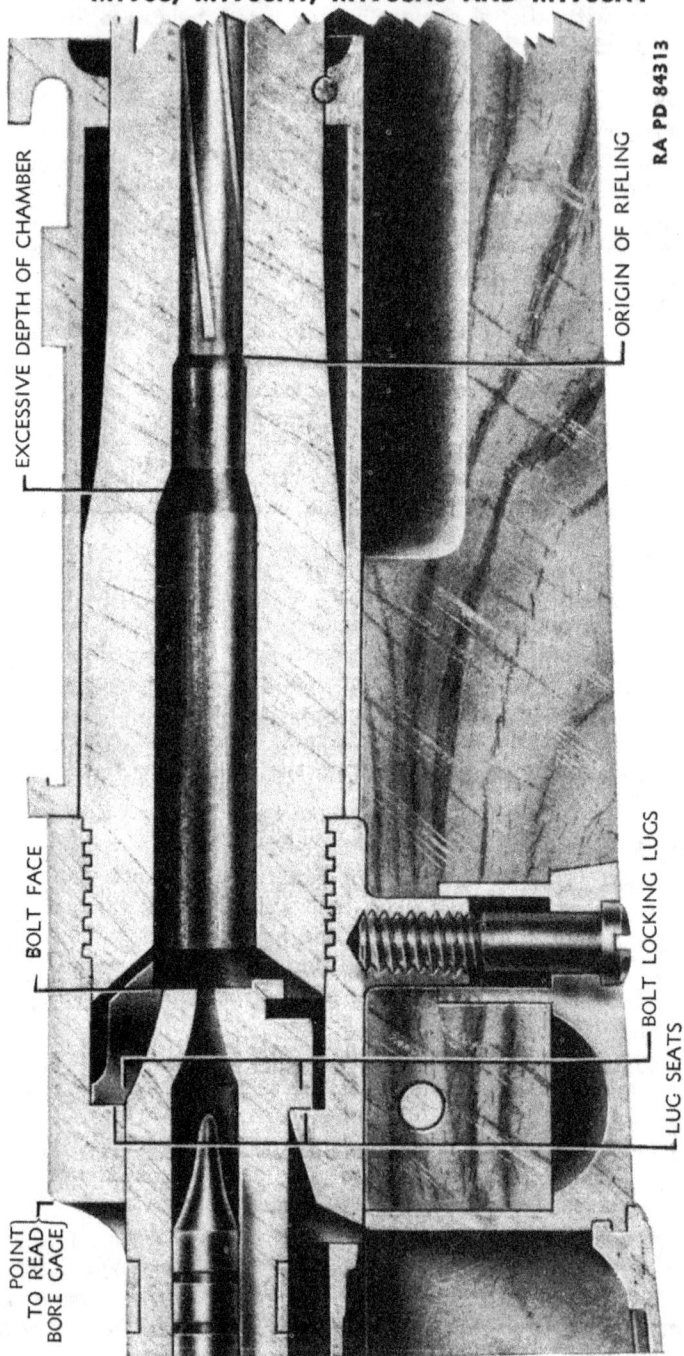

RA PD 84313

*Figure 61 — Points of Wear Determined by Gages — Section
Through Forward End of Receiver and Rear End of Barrel — Vertical View*

INSPECTION

lever. This latter procedure will prevent the use of excessive force. If it does close, replace the bolt of the rifle with the field test bolt and try closing the field test bolt on the headspace gage. If the field test bolt does not close on the gage, a worn bolt is indicated. In this case, the worn bolt will be replaced by a serviceable bolt. If the field test bolt does close on the gage, a worn chamber or worn bolt locking lug seats in the receiver (fig. 61) are indicated. In this case, the rifle will be withdrawn from service and sent to an arsenal for overhaul.

(2) When rifles are being cleaned and repaired at an arsenal or depot, the 1.946- and 1.940-inch gages will be used. The bolt should not close freely on the 1.946-inch gage and should close freely on the 1.940-inch gage.

c. **Trigger Pull.**

(1) Trigger pull for rifles in service must be greater than 3 pounds but should not exceed 6 pounds. Rifles cleaned and repaired in ordnance establishments should have a minimum trigger pull of not less than 3½ pounds. This is to allow for wear.

(2) The inspector, in testing trigger pull of rifles in the hands of troops, should have two weights, one of 3 pounds and one of 6 pounds. Each of these weights should be provided with a wire so that the weight may be suspended from the middle of the bow of the trigger. The wire should be somewhat longer than the distance from the trigger to the butt plate and should have an L-shaped hook on the free end so that, when suspended from the trigger, the weight will hang freely when the barrel of the rifle is vertical.

(3) To test for trigger pull, cock the rifle and turn the safety to "ready." Insert the hook of the trigger weight wire over the middle of the bow of the trigger from the side of the rifle opposite the bolt handle, with the weight resting on the floor and the wire clear of the stock and trigger guard (fig. 62). Then, with the barrel of the rifle held vertically, raise the weight from the floor as gently as possible. If the 3-pound weight pulls the trigger, or if the 6-pound weight fails to pull the trigger, the rifle should be repaired in the manner described in paragraph 47 f (2). For the purpose of inspection of rifles undergoing repair by the Ordnance Department, a 3½-pound weight should be used instead of the 3-pound weight, because all rifles cleaned and overhauled by the Ordnance Department should have a minimum trigger pull of 3½ pounds.

NOTE: Present standard trigger pull test weights are designed to give weights of 3 and 5½ pounds. Weights should be improvised to test for 3 to 6 pounds as now required.

(4) "Creep" is any movement of the trigger that can be felt by the finger after the slack is taken up and before enough pressure is applied to release the sear. Creep should be eliminated as much as possible, whenever found, as it prevents the proper squeeze of the trigger, which is essential to the proper firing of the rifle.

ORDNANCE MAINTENANCE — U.S. RIFLES, CAL. .30,
M1903, M1903A1, M1903A3 AND M1903A4

RA PD 84300

Figure 62 — Testing Trigger Pull

d. Rifle Bore. Inspection of rifle barrels for serviceability will, in general, be based on accuracy, and inspectors will be guided by this requirement. Accuracy is reduced in varying degrees by the following defects: bulges, erosion, and pits. The extent to which these defects in the bore reduce accuracy is determined by two methods: visual inspection and bore gaging. Before any attempt is made to inspect a barrel for serviceability, metal fouling and all other fouling should be removed and the bore wiped dry.

(1) VISUAL INSPECTION.

(a) Place the barrel reflector in the receiver and examine the bore from the muzzle and breech.

(b) If the barrel is not bent or otherwise deformed, the bore appears free from bulges and pits, and the lands are sharp and uniformly distinct, it is serviceable.

(c) If the bore contains small pits but has sharp and uniformly distinct lands and is free from bulges and not otherwise deformed, it is serviceable.

(d) If the barrel contains a bulge, it is unserviceable and should be scrapped. This condition is indicated by a shadowy depression or dark ring in the bore and may often be noticed through a bulge or raised ring on the barrel surface.

(e) If the barrel is pitted to the extent that the sharpness of the

INSPECTION

lands is affected, or if it has a pit or pits in the lands or grooves large enough to permit the passage of gas past the bullet, that is, a pit the width of a land or groove and ⅜ to ½ inch or longer, it is or soon will be, too inaccurate for serviceability and should be scrapped.

(f) During the inspection of the bore from the breech, special attention should be given to the chamber. Fine pits will cause heavy bolt lift and retard rapid fire; large pits may cause the fired cartridge case to stick in the chamber sufficiently to cause failures to extract. Rifles that have pits large enough to cause cartridges to stick in the chamber should be considered unserviceable.

(2) BORE GAGING. The breech bore gage will be used to determine the unserviceability of the weapon due to wear on the lands of the barrel. With the bolt withdrawn, insert the gage through the bolt tunnel and chamber into the bore at the breech, seat gage without undue force, and read the graduation parallel with the top rear edge of the front end of the receiver (fig. 61). If the gage with nine spaces between the rejection line for machine gun barrels and the rejection line for rifle barrels is used, the barrel is unserviceable when the gage reads 0.308 inch or more. If there are eight spaces between the two rejection lines, the barrel is not unserviceable until the breech bore gage reading is 0.309 inch.

29. BOLT GROUP.

a. **Inspection of Component Parts.** Whether or not the bolt has been found serviceable by headspace determination in accordance with paragraph 28 b, the components of the group must be thoroughly inspected.

b. **Bolt Assembly.** Inspect for burs and wear on locking lugs, cocking cam surface, and safety lug. Look for enlarged striker hole in face of bolt, and loose fitting, deformed extractor collar.

c. **Extractor.** Inspect extractor for looseness on extractor collar, weakness and worn or broken hook.

d. **Firing Pin Assembly.** Inspect for broken firing pin, worn or burred cocking cam, sear notch, and safety lock grooves.

e. **Mainspring.** Check mainspring for functioning, set, and distortion. Free length of spring B146871 is approximately 5⅝ inches.

f. **Striker.** Inspect striker for worn or broken point or joint tips.

g. **Bolt Sleeve Assembly.** Inspect for damaged threads or damaged safety lock plunger groove. Test strength of bolt sleeve lock spring and look for wear or burs on lock. Free length of spring B146881 is 0.41-0.03 inch.

h. **Safety Lock Assembly.** Check action of safety lock on bolt sleeve. Look for damaged cocking piece grooves and missing or worn plunger.

ORDNANCE MAINTENANCE — U.S. RIFLES, CAL. .30,
M1903, M1903A1, M1903A3 AND M1903A4

30. FLOOR PLATE, MAGAZINE SPRING, AND FOLLOWER GROUP.

a. **Floor Plate and Follower.** Inspect for burs and wear on floor plate tenons and on surface and edges of follower.

b. **Magazine Spring.** Check magazine spring for functioning and set and inspect for any deformation; free opening of spring C45034 is $4^{17}\!/_{32}$ plus or minus $\frac{1}{32}$ inches.

c. Check (magazine) follower of Rifles M1903A3 and M1903A4 as above, and for deformation. Same magazine spring is used for all models.

31. STOCK GROUP.

a. **Stock.** Inspect stock for deep scratches, bruises, and splits, especially at stock screws and at rear of tang lug of the receiver.

b. **Upper Band Assembly (Rifles M1903 and M1903A1).** Inspect upper band for burs on bayonet stud, worn or burred screws, and damaged stacking swivel.

c. **Bayonet Stud Band (Rifles M1903A3 and M1903A4).** Inspect bayonet stud band in same manner as upper band in subparagraph b, above.

d. **Stacking Swivel Band Assembly (Rifles M1903A3 and M1903A4).** Inspect band for deformation, burs, stripped threads in band and on screw, and security of screw in band. End of screw is expanded to prevent loss, and screw should not be removed except for repairs or replacements. Inspect swivel for deformation.

e. **Lower Band Assembly.** Inspect lower band for worn or burred threads on lower band screw and broken or bent lower band swivel. End of screw is expanded to prevent loss, on (Rifles M1903A3 and M1903A4), and should not be removed except for repairs or replacements.

f. **Lower Band Spring.** Look for loose or weak lower band spring.

g. **Hand Guard Assembly.** Inspect hand guard for splits and missing hand guard clips.

h. **Barrel Guard Assembly (Rifles M1903A3 and M1903A4).** Inspect barrel guard in same manner as hand guard in subparagraph g, above, and for retention in barrel guard ring on barrel. Check barrel guard ring for deformation or burs.

i. **Butt Swivel Assembly.** Look for broken or bent butt swivel and burred or loose swivel screws.

j. **Butt Plate Assembly.** Inspect butt plate assembly for rust, burred or loose butt plate screws, tension of butt plate spring, and broken butt plate cap (or trap, Rifles M1903A3 and M1903A4).

INSPECTION

k. Trigger Guard Group (Rifles M1903 and M1903A1). Inspect for loose or burred guard screws, burred floor plate catch, and weak floor plate catch spring. Free length of spring B146883 is $\frac{5}{16}$ $-\frac{1}{32}$ inch.

l. Trigger Guard Magazine Group (Rifles M1903A3 and M1903A4). Inspect for loose or burred guard screws, loose bushings, cracks or breaks at welds, deformation, and burs. (Bushings are pressed in place and not removable.)

32. BARREL GROUP.

a. Outside Barrel. After barrel has been inspected for serviceability in accordance with paragraph 28 d, inspect the outside for rust, dents, and burs.

b. Front Sight Group (Rifles M1903 and M1903A1). Check alinement of front sight and firmness of movable stud in fixed stud and of fixed stud on barrel. Check for loose or missing front sight screw. Check front sight for shine (par. 46 b (1)).

c. Front Sight Group (Rifle M1903A3). Check alinement of front sight, security of base on barrel, and security of sight and pin in base. There should be no looseness in sight or base. Key should be secure in barrel (par. 46 c). Check front sight for shine (par. 46 b (1)).

d. Rear Sight Assembly (Rifles M1903 and M1903A1). Check rear sight for excessive friction and backlash in windage screw, and for play in rear sight movable base. Check tension of rear sight base spring. Look for loose sight leaf, broken or bent rear sight slide, slide cap, or slide binding screw. Check front and rear overhanging lugs of fixed base for burs and dents.

e. Fixed Base (Rifles M1903 and M1903A1). Check (r e a r sight) fixed base for security on barrel. There should be no looseness.

33. RECEIVER GROUP.

a. General. Inspect receiver for burs and wear on bearing surfaces in well, in locking lug channel, on locking cams and shoulders, cartridge ramp, cocking piece groove, extracting cam, and safety shoulder.

b. Cut-off Assembly. Inspect for burs, missing plunger and spring, weak spring, and loose spindle. Free length of spring B146882 is 0.412-0.044 inch. Check for shine on under side of lower portion where there is a polished surface upon which is impressed the word "ON" (par. 47 b).

c. Bolt Stop Assembly. Inspect for broken or missing spring or pin. (Some Rifles M1903 and M1903A1 are without bolt stop assembly as explained in paragraph 43 i.)

ORDNANCE MAINTENANCE — U.S. RIFLES, CAL. .30, M1903, M1903A1, M1903A3 AND M1903A4

d. **Ejector.**   Inspect for burred or broken point.

e. **Sear.**   Inspect for worn nose and loose sear pin.   Check spring for functioning, fracture, and set.   Free length of spring B146886 is 0.553-0.020 inch.

f. **Trigger.**   Inspect trigger for wear and burs on bearing and heel and check for loose trigger pin.

g. **Rear Sight Assembly (Rifle M1903A3).**   Check security and alinement of rear sight base on receiver, and security of base screw (NOTE, par. 17 f (5)).   Move windage yoke right and left by turning index knob to test smoothness of movement and positioning and tension of windage yoke plunger and spring.   Move slide aperture up and down ramp of windage yoke to test security at various settings and for possible turning movement due to improper assembly or looseness of slide aperture spring (par. 18 f (2)).   Test security of index knob on windage yoke screw and test screw for looseness. Press index knob to left and release to test positive action of index knob spring.   Check wings of sight base and windage yoke for deformation, burs, and rust, and aperture for burs, rust, and foreign matter.

h. **Mount Base (Rifle M1903A4).**

(1) Check mount base for security on receiver, burs, and rust, and screws for security and staking.   Check front mounting recess for wear and burs, and lateral adjusting screws for looseness and burs. (Left lateral adjusting screw should be staked firmly in place and right screw should turn smoothly without undue looseness.)   Check radial grooves in sides of base, and edges of lateral adjusting screws for burs.

(2) Mount the sight to the mount base and check for looseness. There should be no up-and-down movement of the front mount ring in the base when mounted.   Looseness at this point may be remedied by lightly peening the dovetailed lug on the front mount ring (par. 47 h (4)).   Excessive play should be remedied by replacement of parts.

34. TELESCOPIC SIGHT GROUP (RIFLE M1903A4) (figs. 58 and 67).

a. At present the Telescopic Sight M73B1 (Weaver No. 330 C) is furnished for use with the Rifle M1903A4, as described in paragraph 3 d (3).   When issued, a front and rear mount ring are attached to the sight for attaching it to the mount base assembled to the receiver of the rifle.   The mount base is alined, leveled, and screwed to the receiver at manufacture and the screws staked in place.   The base should not be removed nor the left lateral adjusting screw dis-

INSPECTION

turbed unless for adjustment or repair as explained in paragraph 54. Adjustment of the sight is explained in TM 9-270.

b. Adjust the sight for zero windage and elevation as explained in TM 9-270, and mount sight to sight base on rifle. Then bore sight the rifle as explained in paragraph 54, to check alinement of mount base on receiver and sight on mount base.

c. Check the front and rear mount rings for position and security on sight (fig. 8). Check radial grooves in sides of lug on rear mount ring for burs, and dovetailed lug on front ring for wear and burs. There should be no vertical or lateral movement of the front mount ring when mounted.

d. Check sight for dents, rust, cracked, loose, or dirty lenses, loose eyepiece or locking ring. Check for broken or misalined cross hairs in reticle (should run vertical and horizontal). Check for loose screws in adjustment plate. Check for loose elevation or windage screws, worn knurling, and loose locking spring. Figure 67 shows adjustable parts of the sight.

NOTE: Adjustment of cross hairs and sight tube for vertical and horizontal alinement is explained in paragraphs 56 and 58.

e. Check sight for parallax as explained in paragraph 55.

NOTE: There are no spare parts issued for replacement for telescopic sight assemblies. If sight cannot be adjusted as prescribed in this manual, it should be replaced with a new sight assembly, and the damaged sight returned to a base repair shop or factory for repair or disposal. The mount base, shims, front and rear mount rings, and their component screws may be replaced.

35. BAYONET M1905 (figs. 9, 10, and 59).

a. Bayonet as a Unit. Inspect bayonet as a unit for appearance and general condition, fit and positive retention on rifle, and looseness of components.

b. Blade. Inspect blade for deformation, broken or nicked point, nicked or burred blade edge, unserviceable dullness and burs. Check stud ways in handle for wear, dents, burs, and foreign matter. Check scabbard catch well for foreign matter.

c. Guard. Check guard for burs, deformation, deformed or dented barrel band, loose fit on barrel when mounted, looseness on blade, and loose or missing rivets. Check bayonet scabbard catch slot for deformation and burs.

d. Bayonet Catch. Check catch for functioning, wear of hook, free action in slot, deformation, looseness on grip screw, wear in screw hole, and for burs.

e. Scabbard Catch. Check scabbard catch for functioning, free action in well, worn or burred hook, worn knurling, looseness in bayonet catch slot, and for burs. Test spring tension. Free length of catch spring B147063 is 0.475-0.030 inch.

f. Grips. Check grips for cracks, dents, scoring, and protrusion over edge of blade handle. Check grip screw and escutcheons for looseness, wear, projection above grips, and for burs.

36. BAYONET M1 (figs. 11 and 60).

a. Inspect as explained for Bayonet M1905 in paragraph 35.

37. BAYONET SCABBARD M3 (fig. 10).

a. Scabbard as a Unit. Inspect scabbard as a unit for appearance, general condition, fit and retention of bayonet, ease of bayonet withdrawal, and looseness of components.

b. Body. Check body for cuts, deep abrasions, or splitting.

c. Mouthpiece. Check mouthpiece top for looseness in the body and for wear or burs.

d. Hook. Check hook for deformation, wear, and burs.

e. Insert bayonet in scabbard and be sure that *either* latch hook on mouthpiece will engage positively with scabbard catch on bayonet.

38. BAYONET SCABBARD M1910 (fig. 9).

a. Scabbard as a Unit. Inspect scabbard as a unit for appearance, general condition, fit and retention on bayonet, ease of bayonet withdrawal, and looseness of components.

b. Body Cover. Check body cover for condition, cuts, or deep abrasions. Check reinforce leather tip for looseness on body cover due to ripped stitches, cuts, or abrasions, and for condition of leather. Check drain eyelet for security in body and for stoppage and burred flange.

c. Mouthpiece. Check mouthpiece top for looseness in body, catch lugs for deformation and retention by scabbard catch on bayonet. Check for wear and burs. Check bushing for looseness in top, deformation, wear, and burs.

d. Hanger. Check hanger for security, for loose rivet, and for wear or cracking in loop. Check hook for deformation, wear, and burs.

39. BAYONET SCABBARD M7 (fig. 11).

a. Inspect as explained for Bayonet Scabbard M3 in paragraph 37.

INSPECTION

40. GUN SLINGS M1907 AND M1, AND FRONT SIGHT COVER.

a. Gun Sling M1907 (fig. 12).

(1) SLING AS A UNIT. Inspect sling as a unit for appearance, general condition, flexibility, and functioning of hooks, loops, and keepers.

(2) STRAPS (LONG AND SHORT). Check straps for condition of leather, weakness, ripped stitches, cuts, and abrasions. Check hook holes for wear and breaks between holes. Check for tears at rivets, and wear and cracking at loops. Leather straps should not crack when bent at a sharp angle.

(3) HOOKS AND LOOPS. Check hooks for deformation, pinching, and burs. Check rivets for looseness. Check loops for deformation and burs. Check sliding metal keepers for looseness on straps and pinching. (If sliding keepers are of leather, check for ripped stitches.)

b. Gun Sling M1 (fig. 12).

(1) SLING AS A UNIT. Inspect sling as a unit for appearance, general condition, and functioning of keeper buckle and security of hook when assembled to rifle.

(2) BODY. Check body (webbing) for cuts, chafing, or weak spots and indications of rotting. Check clip on end for cracks or insecurity.

(3) HOOK, LOOP, BUCKLE, AND KEEPER. Check hook for cracks or spreading; it should snap onto butt (sling) swivel of rifle and be firmly retained. Check loop and buckle for deformation, burs, and cracks. Check keeper assembly for dents, cracks, and positive retention of body when locked.

c. Front Sight Cover (fig. 13). Check front sight cover for dents, burs, cracks, and shine. Test retention on rifle by snapping cover over front sight with sloping surface to rear. Cover should be firmly retained in position by spring action and without shake or looseness.

ORDNANCE MAINTENANCE — U.S. RIFLES, CAL. .30,
M1903, M1903A1, M1903A3 AND M1903A4

Section IV
MAINTENANCE AND REPAIR

41. GENERAL.

a. Maintenance and repair of the rifles covered in this manual, and their appendages and accessories, consists primarily of replacement of worn or broken parts. These parts are listed in SNL B-3, and symbols are used to indicate whether they are supplied for replacement purposes to the using arms, ordnance maintenance companies, field service shops, or other ordnance establishments. For detailed instructions on disassembly and assembly of this materiel, refer to section II of this manual.

b. Where parts, assemblies, or parts of assemblies are broken or so worn as to render them unserviceable, they must be replaced from stock. Often only parts of assemblies will be worn or broken; where it takes more time to remove the serviceable parts from the assembly than the parts are worth, the assembly should be scrapped.

c. In general, maintenance operations are of a first-aid nature. They are performed with only the limited tool facilities afforded by repair trucks, by semipermanent shops at posts and camps, or by an inspector while making a regular inspection. The decision as to the

MAINTENANCE AND REPAIR

work to be performed by the available personnel with the facilities at hand is left to the discretion of the ordnance officer in charge.

d. The telescopic sight furnished with the Rifle M1903A4 and covered in this manual is issued as a complete assembly. If sight is damaged or cannot be adjusted for serviceability as explained in this manual, it must be replaced with a complete sight assembly and the unserviceable sight returned to a base shop or the factory for repair or disposition. The mount base, mount rings, shims and component screws are replaceable.

42. TOOLS FOR MAINTENANCE AND REPAIR.

a. General Tools. General tools used in maintenance and repair are listed in SNL B-3 as company accessories for the rifle. They are also listed in SNL B-20 and are carried on the small arms repair truck. These tools require no explanation of their use.

b. Special Tools. Special tools used for maintenance and repair are listed and shown in SNL B-20 and are carried on the small arms repair truck. A general description of these tools is given below:

(1) DEVICE, TIGHTENING, FRONT SIGHT, C3826. This device is used for tightening the front sight movable stud when it is loose in the fixed stud (Rifles M1903 and M1903A1). It consists of a pair of tweezers for squeezing together the two sides of the undercut slot on the fixed stud, and a dovetail tapered gage A13220 which, when inserted in the slot of the fixed stud, serves as a stop for the tweezers at the desired point. For details of the use of this device, see paragraph 46 b (3).

(2) ROD, DRILL. The drill rod is a round rod 0.281 inch in diameter and 2.5 feet long. It is provided for removing cleaning rods, cut patches, etc., which may become stuck in the bore of the rifle.

(3) WRENCH, WINDAGE SCREW, SA2822. The windage screw wrench is in the form of a crank, and has a wooden handle. The socket can be adjusted to fit tightly on the knob of the windage screw. It is used for turning the windage screw when disassembling and assembling the rear sight movable base (Rifles M1903 and M1903A1).

43. BOLT GROUP.

a. Bolt Assembly. Burs on lugs and camming surfaces should be removed with a sharpening stone and finished with CLOTH, crocus, care being taken not to remove too much metal. If the striker hole or the face of the bolt is worn or eroded to the extent that it allows the primer of the cartridge to blow back, or tend to blow back, the bolt assembly should be replaced. If the extractor collar is deformed to the extent of affecting the action of the extractor, the bolt assembly should be replaced.

b. Extractor. If the extractor is weak or the hook is broken, it should be replaced.

c. Firing Pin Assembly. Burs on cams, sear notch, and safety lock grooves should be removed with a sharpening stone and finished with CLOTH, crocus. Care should be taken not to deform the sharp edge of the sear notch.

d. Mainspring. If mainspring is weak or will not function properly, it should be replaced.

e. Striker. If striker point is worn or broken or if joint tips are broken, it should be replaced.

f. Bolt Sleeve Assembly. If threads or safety lock plunger groove is deformed, the sleeve should be replaced. Burs on sleeve lock should be removed with a sharpening stone. A weak lock spring should be replaced.

g. Safety Lock Assembly. If safety lock assembly is damaged so that it will not function properly, it should be replaced.

h. Working in Stiff Bolt.

(1) When the bolt fails to function smoothly, it may be worked in by the proper application of COMPOUND, valve grinding, fine (SNL K-2), to the extracting cam and cocking cam, and OIL, lubricating, preservative, special (SNL K-1), to the extractor collar as described in steps (2), (3), and (4), below.

(2) SMOOTHING EXTRACTING CAM (fig. 63). Strip down rifle to receiver, barrel, and bolt. Remove firing pin group from bolt. Place receiver with barrel attached in bench vise, using either wood or leather between vise jaws to prevent damage to rifle. Muzzle and chamber of the barrel should be plugged with CLOTH, wiping, and muzzle end of barrel should be slightly elevated in vise. Apply a small quantity of COMPOUND, valve grinding, fine, to the primary extracting cam situated at the left rear end of receiver (fig. 28). Enter bolt in receiver. Apply COMPOUND, valve grinding, fine, to extracting cam of bolt (fig. 17). Grasp handle of bolt in palm of right hand and, with a forward pressure upon bolt handle, rotate handle rapidly back and forth, at the same time maintaining enough forward pressure upon bolt to keep cam surfaces of receiver and bolt in contact. Continue this operation until a smooth, regular surface is obtained upon both cam surfaces. Wipe dry and thoroughly clean all traces of COMPOUND, valve grinding, fine, from all surfaces of bolt and receiver.

(3) SMOOTHING COCKING CAM (fig. 64). Reassemble firing pin group to bolt. Apply a small quantity of the COMPOUND, valve grinding, fine, to cocking cam surfaces of bolt (fig. 18) and cocking piece (fig. 24). Enter bolt in receiver. Close bolt. *Be sure that trigger and sear are removed from receiver.* Grasp bolt handle in

MAINTENANCE AND REPAIR

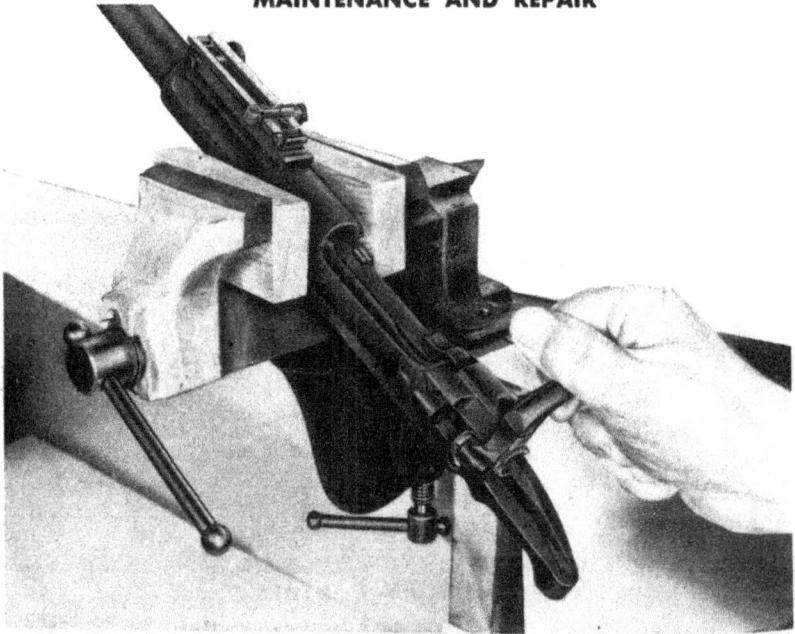

RA PD 10874

Figure 63 — Smoothing Extracting Cam

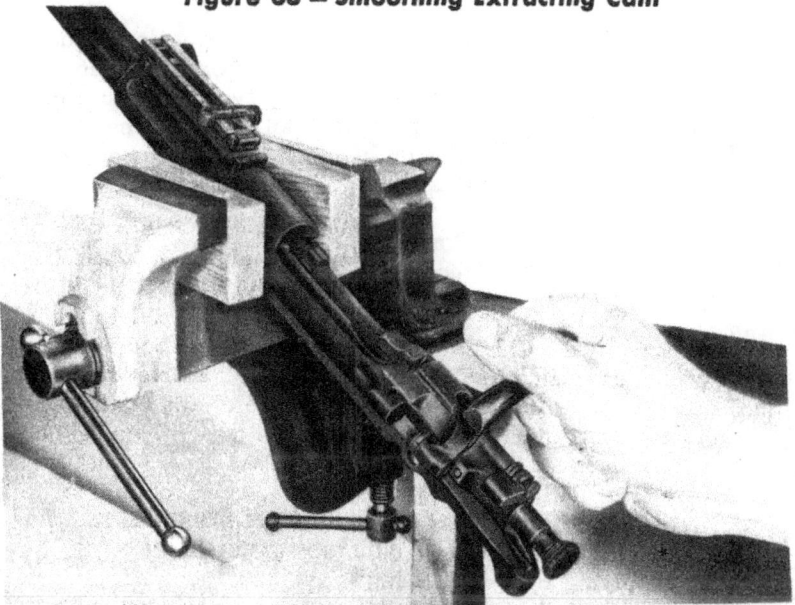

RA PD 10873

Figure 64 — Smoothing Cocking Cam

**ORDNANCE MAINTENANCE — U.S. RIFLES, CAL. .30,
M1903, M1903A1, M1903A3 AND M1903A4**

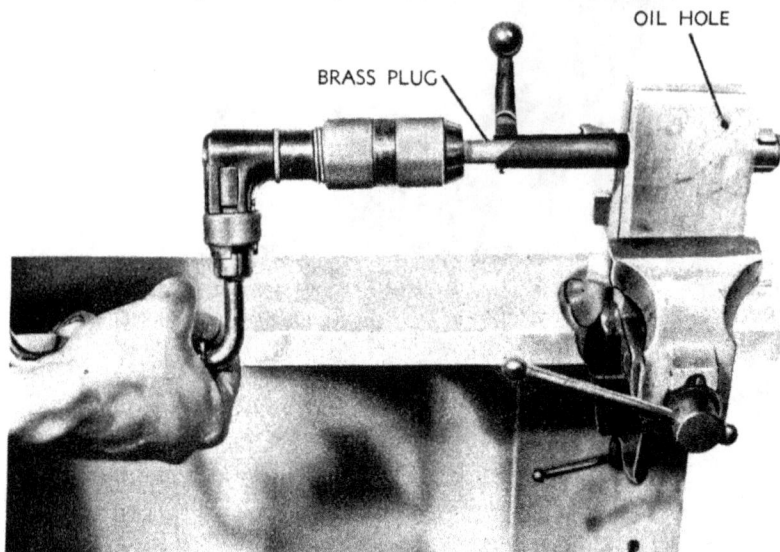

Figure 65 — Working in Extractor Collar RA PD 10862

palm of right hand, and with a slight forward pressure upon bolt handle, rapidly cock and release firing pin by rotating bolt handle up and
down. Continue this operation until a satisfactory smooth surface is
obtained. Clean, dry, and thoroughly wash all traces of the COM-
POUND, valve grinding, fine, from all surfaces, as it is very important
that no trace remain to cause undue wear and injury to the
mechanism.

(4) FREEING EXTRACTOR COLLAR (fig. 65). Provide a pair of
special hardwood jaws with a recess to engage ears of extractor collar
and clearance for body of extractor collar (figs. 17 and 18). Place
jaws in vise, inserting bolt so that ears on extractor collar fall in
dogging slot provided. Close vise with jaws encircling body of bolt,
allowing bolt to be rotated freely while the collar is held stationary. A
¼-inch hole should be drilled in the hardwood vise jaws to allow for
insertion of the lubricating material. Prepare a soft brass plug, one
end turned and threaded to screw into rear end of bolt, the other end,
either square or round, to be gripped by any suitable rotating mem-
ber, preferably a bit brace or breast drill. With brass plug screwed
into bolt and gripped by jaws of bit brace or breast drill, rapidly
rotate bolt, applying freely OIL, lubricating, preservative, special,
only, until extractor collar is entirely free. Clean, wash, and dry bolt.

CAUTION: Special precautions should be taken to remove completely all traces of the COMPOUND, valve grinding, fine, from the

rifle. All washing and cleansing operations should be performed with the barrel held in a vertical position.

i. Bolts Without Bolt Stop Pin Notches.

(1) Some bolts for the M1903 and M1903A1 Rifles do not have notches for the bolt stop pin (fig. 16). These notches were purposely omitted so that the bolt stop assembly (fig. 56) could be eliminated. Whenever a new bolt, which does not have notches, is installed in a Rifle M1903 or M1903A1, it is necessary to remove and discard the bolt stop assembly.

(2) To remove the bolt stop assembly, disassemble the barrel and receiver group from the stock assembly. There is a small hole in one end of the bolt stop spring. Place the end of a pointed instrument in the hole and extract the bolt stop assembly (par. 17 e).

NOTE: The bolt stop assembly is located in the under side of the receiver, directly to the rear of the magazine opening (fig. 56). The bolt stop pin notches in the bolt, are located in the left side of the upper lug on the forward end of the bolt (fig. 16).

44. FLOOR PLATE GROUP (RIFLES M1903 AND M1903A1).

a. Floor Plate and Follower. Burs on floor plate tenons and follower should be removed with a sharpening stone.

b. If magazine spring is weak or damaged, it should be replaced.

45. STOCK GROUP.

a. Stock.

(1) If the stock is split, it should be replaced. Scratches and bruises that do not weaken the stock can be removed or smoothed with a half-round smooth file, and finished with PAPER, flint, class B, No. 00.

(2) DISTORTION.

(a) It is frequently found that stocks are distorted due to moisture, a condition which makes their assembly to barrel and receiver assemblies difficult. The stock should fit the rifle snugly at only two points, namely, in the immediate vicinity of the front and rear guard screws. The recoil lug of the receiver fits into a mortise in the stock, and the front guard screw which is screwed into the lug holds the stock firmly between the guard and the forward under surface of the receiver. The portion of the stock forward of this point is so designed that the barrel floats freely in it without actually being supported by it and sufficient clearance is allowed so that it does not bind when the barrel becomes heated. The barrel bed or the extreme forward end of the stock upon which the upper (or bayonet stud) band is assembled is the most critical point. "Bound barrels" occur frequently. A bound barrel does not have room for expansion when heated during firing and may become warped, bulged, or twisted.

ORDNANCE MAINTENANCE — U.S. RIFLES, CAL. .30, M1903, M1903A1, M1903A3 AND M1903A4

(b) If this condition is caused by too much wood on the stock, remove upper band screw and slip off the upper band (Rifles M1903 and M1903A1). Polish off that portion of the stock on which the upper band seats with PAPER, flint, class B, No. 00. After a little wood has been removed, a small file should be used to square up the shoulder for the upper band. As the work progresses, the upper band should be put in place without the insertion of the upper band screw and the barrel tested for looseness by a vertical motion. The foregoing operation should be repeated until there is a perceptible movement of the barrel when the upper band is assembled on the gun. It sometimes becomes necessary to remove some stock from the front tenon of the hand guard. This stock can be removed with PAPER, flint, class B, No. 00.

(c) If the condition is caused by the upper band screw being too far from the barrel bed, remove the upper band screw, slip off the upper band, and plug up the upper band screw hole. Replace upper band and establish center of new hole for upper band screw so that there will be a perceptible movement of the barrel when the upper band is assembled on the gun. Drill out the new hole and assemble upper band and upper band screw in place.

(d) If both of above methods fail, the barrel bed should be gouged out very slightly with a rasp, file, or similar tool until the barrel floats satisfactorily. The float in the barrel may be checked by placing thumb on under side of barrel and forefinger on top of upper band and exerting pressure on the barrel. The barrel should spring away from stock when a pressure of approximately 4 pounds is exerted.

NOTE: The same general procedure can be followed for the bayonet stud band, stacking swivel band, and barrel guard of the Rifles M1903A3 and M1903A4.

(3) MAGAZINE WELL. If trigger guard (or trigger guard magazine) will not assemble properly with barrel and receiver assembly, a wood rasp is used to remove the interference. This must be done carefully to avoid removing too much wood. It is necessarily a cut and try operation and should be done only by personnel familiar with this type of work.

b. **Upper Band Assembly (Rifles M1903 and M1903A1).** Burs on bayonet stud should be removed with a sharpening stone. Burs on screwheads should be removed with a fine file. If threads are burred, they should be chased with a die. If stacking swivel is bent, it can probably be straightened by placing it in a vise with copper jaws and bending it back into shape, using a hammer, wrench, or cold chisel. If it cannot be bent back into shape, or if it is broken, it should be replaced.

NOTE: The same general procedure can be followed for the bayonet stud band of the Rifles M1903A3 and M1903A4. If the stacking swivel is bent and cannot be easily straightened without disassembling from the band, the stacking swivel band assembly should be replaced.

c. **Lower Band Assembly.** Burs on screw threads should be removed with a die. A broken or bent swivel should be treated as described in subparagraph b, above. (The lower band screw of the Rifles M1903A3 and M1903A4 is expanded at the end to prevent removal. If screw, band, or swivel are damaged, the assembly should be replaced.)

d. **Lower Band Spring.** A damaged lower band spring should be replaced.

e. **Hand Guard or Barrel Guard Assembly.** A split hand guard or barrel guard should be replaced.

f. **Butt Swivel Assembly.** Burs on screwheads should be removed with a fine file. Loose screws should be tightened. A broken or bent swivel should be treated as in subparagraph b, above. (If the swivel on Rifles M1903A3 and M1903A4 is damaged, the assembly should be replaced.)

g. **Butt Plate Assembly.** Burs on butt plate and screwheads should be removed with a fine file. Loose screws should be tightened. A weak or broken butt plate spring should be replaced (Rifles M1903 and M1903A1). If the butt plate trap spring of Rifles M1903A3 and M1903A4 is weak or broken, the butt plate assembly should be replaced.

h. **Trigger Guard Group (Rifles M1903 and M1903A1).** Burs on screwheads should be removed with a fine file. Damaged threads should be chased with a die. A broken floor plate catch or weak spring should be replaced.

i. **Trigger Guard Magazine Group (Rifles M1903A3 and M1903A4).** Burs on screwheads should be removed with a fine file. Damaged threads should be chased with a die. If threads are worn so as to make screws loose, screws should be replaced.

46. BARREL GROUP.

a. Rust should be removed from the outside of the barrel by rubbing with a CLOTH, wiping in OIL, lubricating, preservative, special. If this is not sufficient, lightly use CLOTH, crocus, taking care not to produce a shiny surface. Burs should be removed with a sharpening stone.

b. **Front Sight Group (Rifles M1903 and M1903A1)** (fig. 51).

(1) If front sight is bent, broken, or shiny, it should be replaced. If movable stud is damaged, it should be replaced. The fixed stud is supplied as a component of the barrel assembly.

NOTE: In an emergency, shine may be eliminated temporarily in a manner similar to that prescribed for the cut-off in NOTE, paragraph 47 b.

(2) To repair a loose front sight fixed stud, drive out fixed stud pin and remove fixed stud. Slightly peen the top surface of the spline on the barrel. The peening should be just enough to make a snug fit between the slot in the fixed stud and the spline when assembled. Reassemble fixed stud and fixed stud pin.

(3) To tighten a loose movable stud in fixed stud, the front sight tightening device C3826 is the standard tool for use in the field. To use the device, the front sight screw and movable stud are removed and the dovetailed gage A13220 inserted in place of the movable stud, being pushed in by hand until tight. It is then withdrawn sufficiently to allow the fixed stud to be closed to the correct dimension. It will be noted in this connection that the dovetailed gage acts as a stop in closing the fixed stud. The tweezers are then applied and the fixed stud closed to its original size and shape to fit the movable stud. The amount the gage is withdrawn depends on the amount the fixed stud is sprung. This can be estimated very accurately, after a little practice, by noting the amount of looseness of the sight before attempting to use the device. Replace movable stud and screw in front sight screw.

(4) When new movable studs are installed, it may be found necessary to drill a hole for the front sight screw, as considerable quantities of undrilled movable studs of early manufacture are still in stock. To drill this hole proceed as follows: Locate the movable stud centrally in the fixed stud. With the muzzle of the rifle held firmly in a vise, copper jaws being used, and the butt of the rifle supported on the bench, drill a hole 0.0935 inch in diameter in the movable stud approximately $\frac{3}{16}$ inch deep, using the hole already drilled in the fixed stud as a jig or guide. Care must be taken not to bur the threads in the fixed stud. Keep the drill well oiled. Put little pressure on the drill until it has been well started or the drill may be broken or the movable stud moved. After the hole has been drilled, it should be reamed out with a 0.094-inch reamer, care being taken not to put too much weight on the reamer as it is inclined to wedge and break. It may be possible that the threads for the front sight screw are burred and should be cleaned out with the 0.117-inch tap; this can be determined by screwing the front sight screw into the fixed stud.

c. **Front Sight Group, Rifle M1903A3** (fig. 54). In this rifle, the base of the front sight which corresponds to the fixed stud in subparagraph b, above, is held on the barrel by a key seated in a longitudinal keyway, and a pin passing through the sight base and a groove in the key when assembled. If the key is worn, it should be replaced.

MAINTENANCE AND REPAIR

If keyway in barrel is worn it may be peened in slightly at the top edges or at the ends. There should be no movement of the key in the keyway when assembled. If the front sight (blade) is loose, bent, broken, or shiny, it should be replaced, using same height of sight as the one removed (NOTE, subpar. b (1), above). (There are several heights of front sight used, as listed in SNL B-3.)

d. Rear Sight Assembly (Rifles M1903 and M1903A1).

(1) It is important that the front and rear lips of the rear sight movable base fit snugly in the undercuts of the fixed base. This is necessary so that the rear sight leaf when raised does not rock from side to side in a manner that may cause errors in sighting from round to round, and so that the movable base will remain in the proper position when "windage" is taken by the firer. Looseness of the movable base can usually be corrected by tapping either one or both of the overhanging lugs of the fixed base (ordinarily the rear one), using a bronze block or a drift so that the lug is bent slightly. If these undercuts of the fixed base are burred or bind the movable base too tightly, the movable base should be removed and the shaving tools 24-17-9C and 24-17-9D for the front and rear ends of the rear sight fixed base, used (when available) to shave the surface to a proper fit.

(2) The windage screw is handled as an assembly, for when the spring is weakened the threads are generally worn also, and it is practical to replace the entire assembly.

(3) A bent rear sight slide is corrected by using a face plate or other flat surface, a set with a face approximately $\frac{7}{16}$ by $\frac{5}{8}$ inch, and a small hammer. The straightness is gaged by the use of a scale. The slide should be very slightly concave.

(4) A bent rear sight slide cap, pin, binding screw, rear sight leaf, or weak base spring is corrected by replacing the proper part or parts. The fixed base is supplied as a component of the barrel assembly.

47. RECEIVER GROUP.

a. Burs on bearing surfaces and cams of receiver should be removed with a sharpening stone, taking care not to remove too much metal, nor to change the angle of the face.

b. Cut-off Assembly. A broken cut-off, spring, plunger, or spindle should be replaced. If cut-off screw will not retain the spindle, it should be replaced. If the under side of the lever portion of the cut-off where the word "ON" is stamped (fig. 23) is shiny, the cut-off should be replaced, when possible, by one with an oxide black finish. When rifles are being overhauled and this part is given an oxide black finish it should be left *black*, and not repolished. All cut-off levers used for replacement and on hand should be given a black finish to eliminate this shiny finish.

ORDNANCE MAINTENANCE — U.S. RIFLES, CAL. .30, M1903, M1903A1, M1903A3 AND M1903A4

NOTE: In an emergency, shine may be eliminated temporarily by the application of PAINT, black, flat, to the shiny surface. The surface should be thoroughly cleaned to remove all oil and dirt before applying paint. Such painting should be considered only as a temporary correction as the paint will soon wear off.

c. **Bolt Stop Assembly.** If parts are broken or spring is weak, assembly should be replaced. (Some Rifles M1903 and M1903A1 are without the bolt stop assembly, as explained in paragraph 43 i.)

d. **Ejector.** Burs on the point of the ejector should be removed with a sharpening stone.

e. **Sear.** Burs on nose of sear should be removed with a sharpening stone, taking care to remove as little metal as possible and to retain the proper angle of the faces. If nose is worn so that it will not hold in sear notch of firing pin, sear should be replaced. A weak or damaged spring should be replaced. If the sear pin is worn sufficiently to allow side play, it should be replaced.

f. **Trigger.**

(1) Burs on bearing and heel of trigger should be removed with a sharpening stone, care being taken not to remove too much metal. A loose trigger pin, especially if it allows side play, should be replaced.

(2) When creep, as defined in paragraph 28 c (4) is found in a trigger, or when the trigger weight does not fall within the prescribed limits, examine the sear nose and sear notch for burs or rough surfaces (fig. 66). All burs should be removed by stoning and all surfaces which are not perfectly smooth should be polished by stoning. *Sharp corners and edges must not be rounded off.* Should this procedure fail to produce the desired degree of smoothness in the action or the desired correction in trigger weight, the heel of the trigger and the point at which it comes in contact with the receiver should be inspected and any roughness removed by stoning. Should the action still be faulty, it will be necessary to interchange the parts until a combination of cocking piece, sear and sear spring, trigger, and mainspring is found which will correct the difficulty. The probable importance of these various parts in the perfection of the trigger pull is in the order given. A number of parts should be tried in their various combinations until a satisfactory pull is obtained. The shapes of the cocking piece sear notch and sear nose and the strength of the sear spring should always be such that the sear invariably rises to its full height and the trigger returns to its forward position on a cocked rifle when the trigger is released.

g. **Rear Sight Assembly, Rifle M1903A3** (fig. 57). If aperture slide, spring, or screw are damaged so as to prevent proper operation or retention of the slide, the damaged parts should be replaced.

MAINTENANCE AND REPAIR

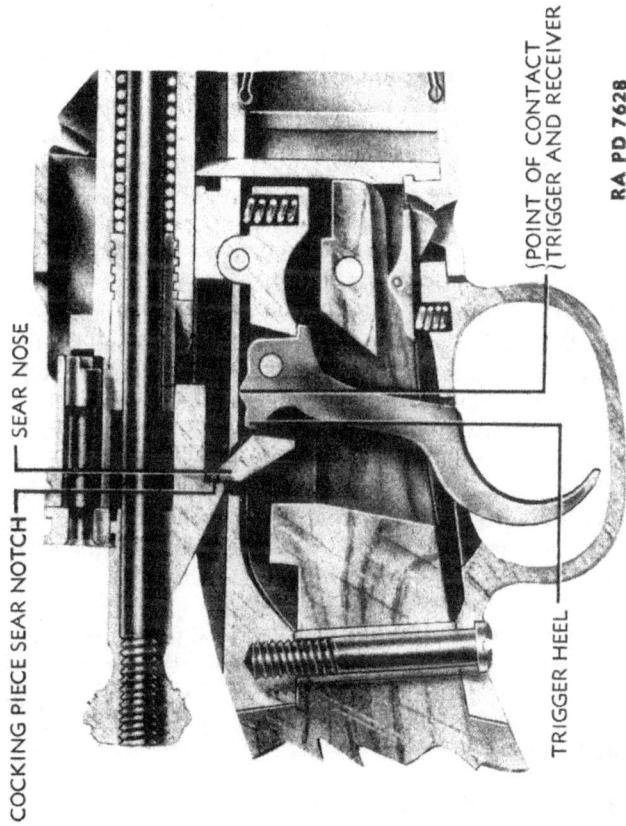

Figure 66 — Trigger and Sear Mechanism — Section Through Rear End of Receiver — Vertical View

RA PD 7628

COCKING PIECE SEAR NOTCH

SEAR NOSE

POINT OF CONTACT TRIGGER AND RECEIVER

TRIGGER HEEL

If the windage index knob screw or spring are damaged, they should be replaced. If other parts of the sight assembly other than springs or screws are damaged, the rear sight assembly should be replaced. Burs on threads of windage yoke screw may be removed with a die.

NOTE: Improper assembly of the slide aperture spring may cause the slide aperture to operate poorly, as explained in paragraph 33 g.

h. Telescopic Sight Group, Rifle M1903A4.

(1) The Telescopic Sight M73B1 (Weaver No. 330 C) is issued as a complete assembly and aside from cleaning, oiling, and adjustments prescribed in paragraphs 55, 56, 57, 58, and 60, no repairs can be made in the field. If the sight becomes unserviceable it should be replaced by a new sight assembly and the damaged one forwarded to a base shop (or the factory) for repair or disposition.

(2) The mount base and mount rings, together with their component screws and shims, are replaceable. When such parts are replaced, the sight should be checked for alinement and level, as prescribed in paragraphs 57 and 58.

(3) If the mounting recess in the front end of the mount base becomes burred, it may be smoothed by using a small file or sharpening stone. If the recess becomes enlarged to the extent that the front mount ring has play, the base should be replaced. (Such play may result from a worn mounting lug on the front mount ring.)

(4) If the mounting lug on the front mount ring becomes burred it may be smoothed with a small file or sharpening stone. When wear is present to the extent that there is play between ring and base, it may sometimes be tightened by lightly peening the ends of the lug towards the ring. If such peening does not take up the slack, the ring should be replaced. (Such looseness may be due to wear in the mounting recess in the base.) Before peening the lug, the front mount ring should be removed from the sight and mounted on a metal rod of the same diameter as the sight tube, to prevent deformation of the ring when peening. *Never attempt to peen the ring while mounted on the sight.*

48. BAYONET M1905.

a. Nicks and Burs. Nicks and burs on metal parts should be smoothed with a fine grained sharpening stone. Burs and scratches on wood grips should be smoothed with a fine flat file. The point of the blade should be kept serviceably sharp. Dents in edges of blade can often be peened out before smoothing.

b. Loose Rivet in Guard. Peen rivets or punch out and replace with new rivets and peen; file heads flush with fine flat file. Take care not to make a shiny spot on guard, which may reflect light.

c. Worn Stud Ways. When stud ways are worn sufficiently to

MAINTENANCE AND REPAIR

make loose fit of bayonet on file, the ways may be peened sufficiently to make fit secure. Peening should be done lightly and bayonet fitted to stud frequently during process.

d. Dry Grips. When wood of grips shows signs of dryness, OIL, linseed, raw, should be applied, allowed to soak in thoroughly, and the grips then wiped clean. Occasional light applications of this oil help to keep wood in condition, especially in dry climates. Care should be taken to keep oil from getting into slots and apertures of metal parts, as it will become gummy when dry. The grips should be dismounted when oiling. Cracked grips should be replaced. (Composition grips may be assembled in place of the wood grips.)

e. If bayonet catch or scabbard catch are burred or worn so that they will not hold bayonet or scabbard positively, the face of the catches may sometimes be filed square. If badly worn so as to cause looseness the parts should be replaced.

49. BAYONET M1.

a. This bayonet is the same in construction as the Bayonet M1905 in paragraph 48, and may be repaired in the same manner. However, the grips are of composition and should not be oiled. If grips are cracked or chipped, or escutcheon loose, the grips should be replaced.

50. BAYONET SCABBARD M3.

a. Nicks and Burs. Nicks and burs on mouthpiece top, or top be removed with a smooth file. A flat file with a safe edge should be used for flat surfaces and a rat-tailed file for inside curved surfaces.

b. Top Loose in Body. If the top becomes loose from the body, it may be tightened by springing the lugs of the metal top into the notches provided in the body of the scabbard.

c. If either hook on mouthpiece will not positively engage the scabbard catch on the bayonet, it may be fitted by filing the forward face of the hook slightly. Be sure to file level. Do not file scabbard catch, unless burred or worn uneven.

51. BAYONET SCABBARD M1910.

a. Nicks and Burs. Nicks and burs on mouthpiece top, or top bushing, should be removed with smooth file. A flat file with safe edge should be used for flat surfaces and a rat-tailed file for inside curved surfaces.

b. Top Loose in Body. If top becomes loose in (metal) body, it may sometimes be tightened as follows: Place piece of flat metal in blade opening of top (to prevent springing) and place scabbard on solid edge of flat surface, such as the anvil of a vice, so that rim of top does not contact; then separate cover from rim of top, insert thin cold chisel just back of rim of top, and strike lightly with hammer. The metal body is crimped into a groove in top just back of beveled rim. Care must be taken as main body of scabbard is wood.

c. Scratched or Gouged Leather Reinforce. Rough spots on leather reinforce, caused by scratches or gouges, may be smoothed by paring with sharp, flat blade.

d. Dried-out (Dead) Leather. An occasional cleaning with SOAP, castile, or SOAP, saddle, will help to keep leather from drying out. Do not use oil as it will soak in and discolor the fabric.

52. BAYONET SCABBARD M7.

a. This scabbard is the same in construction as the Scabbard M3 in paragraph 50, except that it is shorter. It may be repaired in the same manner.

53. GUN SLINGS M1907 AND M1, AND FRONT SIGHT COVER.

a. Gun Sling M1907.

(1) Dried-out (Dead) Leather. When straps become dried out, as indicated by light cracking or stiffness, a thorough cleaning with SOAP, saddle, will help condition the leather. A thick lather of soap should be worked well into the leather and rinsed off with clean water. Polish briskly with dry, clean CLOTH, wiping. If this treatment does not soften the leather, apply a very light coating of OIL, neat's-foot.

(2) Scratches and Gouges. When straps become rough from leather "picked up" by scratches, cuts, or gouges, they may be smoothed by paring lightly with a sharp, flat blade.

(3) Bent Sliding Loops and Hooks. When (metal) sliding loops or hooks become spread or pinched, they should be corrected. Loops may be spread by placing a piece of flat metal between loop and strap and using a light hammer.

(4) Worn Holes in Straps. When holes in straps become worn or leather is torn between holes, the strap should be replaced. Punching new holes will weaken strap.

b. Gun Sling M1.

(1) As this sling is made of webbing, repair is not usually practical and, if damaged, it should be replaced as a unit.

(2) Loop and Buckle. If the loop or buckle become bent they may sometimes be straightened by disassembling the sling and tapping bent parts with a hammer to straighten. When tapping, lay part flat on hard, level surface such as the anvil of a vise.

(3) Hook. If the (spring) hook becomes spread, it may be squeezed together until it will hold properly.

(4) Keeper. If the keeper will not clamp the web strap securely

and positively or if metal parts are badly damaged or have cracks, or the webbing is cut or frayed, the sling should be replaced as a unit.

c. Front Sight Cover.

(1) If the front sight cover becomes bent or loose on the front sight when assembled, or if it becomes shiny, it should be replaced.

(2) LOOSENESS. If the sight cover becomes slightly loose when assembled, it may sometimes be tightened by removing it and pressing the curved lower sides together to obtain more spring-gripping action.

(3) SHINE. If the sight cover becomes shiny, it should be replaced or in an emergency the shine removed as explained for the front sight in NOTE, paragraph 46 b (1).

54. BORE SIGHTING, RIFLE M1903A4.

a. General.

(1) The Telescopic Sight M73B1 (Weaver No. 330 C) used on the Rifle M1903A4 is set at zero windage and 100 yards elevation (when issued) as explained in TM 9-270. The mount base is alined and leveled by means of shims of proper thickness placed between mount base and receiver at manufacture. The position of the telescopic sight is fixed at the front end by the engagement of the mounting lug on the front mount ring (assembled to tube of sight) engaging in the mounting recess in the front end of the mount base. The rear end of the sight can be swung to right or left and then locked in position by movement of the lateral adjusting screws threaded into the mount base and bearing on the lug on the rear mount ring. The position of the rear end of the sight is fixed at manufacture by staking the *left* lateral adjusting screw in position. This screw should not be removed nor shifted except for repair or realinement of the sight when necessary. The sight is removed from the mount base by removing the *right* lateral adjusting screw and swinging the rear (eyepiece) end of the sight out from the receiver (bolt handle side) until sight is at right angles to receiver. Then lift sight straight up as explained in paragraph 7 a.

(2) However, if the sight gets out of line with the base and hence the bore, by shifting or removal of the *left* lateral adjusting screw or replacement of rings or mount base, it must be lined up again by bore sighting the rifle as explained below, and the *left* lateral adjusting screw then securely staked in place. By alining the sight with the bore, with the cross hairs (reticle) at zero windage (TM 9-270), maximum adjustment of the cross hairs is retained for windage adjustment by means of the windage adjusting screw. The same principle applies to elevation when the mount base is leveled at manufacture. If mount base is removed or replaced, the sight should be checked for vertical alinement with the bore in a similar manner. In such a case, the mount base can be tipped by placing the shim of

ORDNANCE MAINTENANCE — U.S. RIFLES, CAL. .30,
M1903, M1903A1, M1903A3 AND M1903A4

proper thickness under the front or rear end of the mount base, as may be required. The horizontal cross hair should then pass through the point of aim. Before bore sighting, the sight should be adjusted for zero windage and minimum range of 100 yards as explained in TM 9-270.

b. Bore Sighting.

(1) With the rifle fully unloaded, and sight set at zero windage and 100 yards elevation, as explained in TM 9-720, remove the bolt from the rifle.

(2) Place the rifle on a solid rest and, looking through the bore, aline the center of the bore with a point about 100 yards distant.

(3) Without shifting the rifle, look through the sight and shift the rear end by means of the lateral adjustment screws until the *vertical* (windage) cross hair of the reticle passes through the point of aim.

(4) Tighten both lateral adjusting screws with care not to shift the alinement. Be sure the edges of the screws fit fully into the radial grooves in mount base and rear mount ring lug.

(5) Remove the rifle from the rest and the sight from the mount base, by removing the *right* lateral adjusting screw, and securely stake the *left* lateral adjusting screw in position. This can be done by tapping the mount base directly above the thread of the screw with a small center punch.

NOTE: If the *right* lateral adjusting screw becomes too loose to hold properly, it can be tightened in like manner. Such staking should be light, else thread of screw may be damaged. This screw must be removed to dismount the sight.

(6) If it is necessary to level the mount base, it may be done by loosening the mount base screws and shimming up front or rear end of base until *horizontal* cross hair passes through the point of aim at 100 yards. The shim can then be properly assembled and the mount base screws tightened and staked in position. Mount base screws should be drawn down tightly.

55. PARALLAX ADJUSTMENT OF TELESCOPIC SIGHT M73B1 (WEAVER NO. 330 C).

a. General.

(1) The parallax of the Telescopic Sight M73B1 (Weaver No. 330 C) is adjusted by backward and forward movement of the reticle (cross hairs) attached to the adjustment plate on the sight. Parallax is adjusted at manufacture for 25 yards and beyond, and the plate screwed firmly in place. The plate should never be moved nor the screws allowed to become loose except when adjustment is found to be necessary. If parallax develops, it will cause the cross hairs to become blurred when the target image is in sharp focus. If no parallax exists the cross hairs should be clearly defined when the sight is

MAINTENANCE AND REPAIR

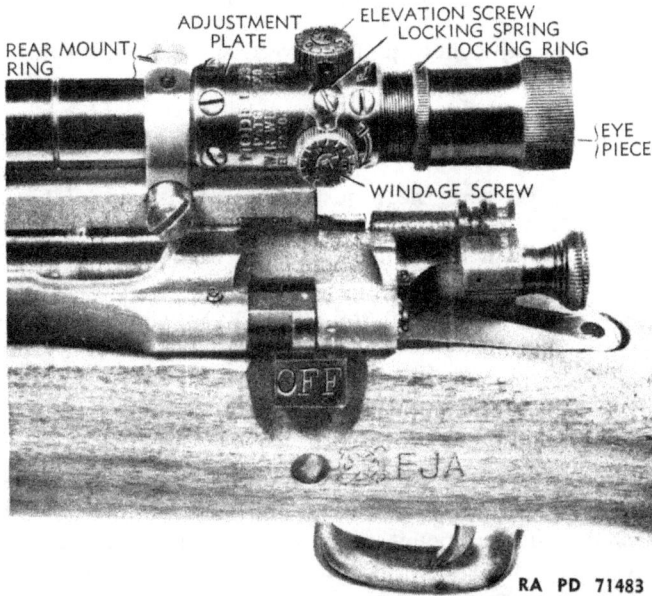

Figure 67 — Telescopic Sight M73B1 (Weaver No. 330 C) — Rear Section Showing Adjusting Screws and Eyepiece

focussed on an object at 25 yards or more distant as described in TM 9-270. However as such a short range is not generally necessary, parallax should not be adjusted if correct for ranges used.

NOTE: The *reticle* in the Telescopic Sight M73B1 (Weaver No. 330 C) consists of a metal ring in which two very fine wires are assembled. These wires cross each other at a right angle and are referred to as the "cross hairs." The reticle is assembled in the sight tube and adjusted by the windage and elevation screws as explained in TM 9-270.

b. **Testing for Parallax.**

(1) Place the sight on a rigid support, focus the sight, and aline the reticle (cross hairs) on a mark about 100 yards distant.

(2) While looking through the sight, move the head from side to side. If there is any apparent movement between the reticle (cross hairs) and the mark, parallax is present.

(3) In the Telescopic Sight M73B1 (Weaver, No. 330 C), parallax may be present at 25 yards or less and not at greater distances. If not present at ranges used, do not adjust.

c. **Adjusting for Parallax.** To eliminate parallax, proceed as follows:

(1) Lightly loosen the four screws holding the adjustment plate (fig. 67).

(2) Slide the adjustment plate forward and back until the reticle (cross hairs) and mark sighted on appear stationary when the head is moved from side to side.

(3) Tighten the adjustment plate by turning down the screws securely.

CAUTION: Be sure the adjustment plate is moved backward or forward *only* and not laterally. If moved laterally, the vertical and horizontal alinement of the reticle will become shifted. Do not remove the adjustment plate from the sight tube as the cross hairs in the reticle are very delicate and easily broken, and foreign matter may enter the sight tube. Loosen adjustment plate screws *only enough* to shift plate, else the curved nuts into which they thread may drop off inside the tube. This applies particularly to single (rear) screw, as nut may turn and break cross hairs.

56. PLACING RETICLE OF TELESCOPIC SIGHT VERTICAL.

a. If the reticle should become shifted in the sight tube, or the tube become shifted in the mount rings, so that the cross hairs are not exactly vertical and horizontal with the mount base and bore line, they may be so positioned by loosening the front and rear mount ring screws and turning the sight in the mount rings, and then tightening the screws. In the Telescopic Sight M73B1 (Weaver No. 330 C) the windage cross hair should be vertical, with the windage screw (stamped "L") on the *left* side of the rifle when in position.

CAUTION: Tighten mount ring screws only enough to hold sight firmly in position. If screws are drawn down too tight, the sight tube may become bent, and the sight thrown out of adjustment or the lenses cracked.

b. If it is not possible to adjust the position of the cross hairs sufficiently, as outlined in subparagraph a, above, further slight adjustment may be made in the case of the Telescopic Sight M73B1 (Weaver No. 330 C), by moving the adjustment plate to *right or left*. This is done by loosening the screws holding the plate as described for parallax adjustment in paragraph 55. Be sure to note CAUTION in paragraph 55 c (3).

CAUTION: Be sure the adjustment plate is not moved backward or forward, else the parallax adjustment will be disturbed.

57. REPLACING MOUNT BASE, RIFLE M1903A4.

a. General. The mount base of this rifle is alined and leveled with respect to the bore line of the rifle to which it is assembled at manufacture, and should not be removed except for repair. If necessary to replace base on account of wear in the front mount ring mounting recess, or other damage, the new base must be leveled with respect to the bore line of the rifle. Lateral alinement of the base

MAINTENANCE AND REPAIR

is fixed by the position of the screw holes in base and receiver for each barrel and receiver assembly. Leveling of the base with respect to the bore line is attained by raising the front or rear end of the base. Metal shims A153174 A, B, C, and D ranging in thickness from 0.005 plus or minus 0.001 inch to 0.020 plus or minus 0.001 inch are provided for this purpose. These shims are inserted between mount base and receiver, at front or rear end, to level the base.

b. Leveling Mount Base. To level the mount base, proceed as follows:

(1) Assemble mount base to receiver without shims, unless proper shim and its position is known. Turn mount base screws down, but not tightly.

(2) Adjust sight to zero windage and 100 yards elevation as described in TM 9-270, and mount sight to mount base.

(3) Bore sight rifle for windage as prescribed in paragraph 54, and note position of *horizontal* cross hair with respect to mark sighted on. If horizontal cross hair is above the mark the *rear* end of the base must be raised. If below the mark, the front end of base must be raised.

(4) Loosen both mount base screws slightly and insert a shim (thinnest first) between mount base and receiver at front or rear end as may be necessary, and tighten screws. Then check position of horizontal cross hair. (Be sure position of rifle is not shifted while inserting shim.) Continue with leveling until proper shim is found; then remove base and assemble shim, and screw base down tightly.

(5) Check alinement and leveling on the range, and when correct stake mount base screws in position.

NOTE: To prevent rusting, oil receiver, mount base, and shim where they contact, before final assembly, using OIL, lubricating, preservative, medium.

58. ADJUSTING MOUNT RINGS ON TELESCOPIC SIGHT.

a. General. The front and rear mount rings of the Telescopic Sight M73B1 (Weaver No. 330 C) are adjusted and clamped to the sight when issued, and should not be removed except for repair. If these rings should become loose or detached while the sight is dismounted from the rifle, they can be assembled to the sight as explained in subparagraph b, below. The proper position of the mount rings with respect to the tube, and the proper position of the assembled sight with respect to the mount base are shown in figures 8 and 5.

b. Assembly and Adjustment of Mount Rings.

(1) Loosen the mount ring screw and slide the narrow, rear mount ring onto the sight tube from the front end and back against the adjustment plate on the rear end of the tube. Turn the ring until the flat face of the lug is on the opposite side of the tube from the elevation

screw marked "UP." Then tighten the mount ring screw sufficiently to hold in position. NOTE, step (4), below.

(2) Slide the board, front mount ring onto the sight tube in a similar manner until the front face of the ring is approximately 3¼ inches from the front end of the sight tube and the flat face of the mounting lug is parallel with the flat face of the lug on the rear mount ring; then, insert the lug on the front mount ring into the undercut recess in the mount base and turn the sight as in mounting (par. 8 d). As the rear mount ring approaches the mount base, move the sight backward or forward in the front mount ring until the rear ring will seat squarely in position on the mount base. Thread in and tighten the *right* lateral adjusting screw to hold the rear mount ring in position, and then partially tighten the two mount ring screws in the front mount ring. Be sure the edges of the cupped heads of the lateral adjusting screws fit squarely in the radial notches in the lug on the rear mount ring and mount base before tightening the front mount ring screws.

CAUTION: Tighten mount ring screws only enough to hold sight firmly in position. If screws are drawn down too tight, the sight tube may become bent, the sight thrown out of adjustment or the lenses cracked.

(3) Dismount and mount the sight to test position of rings. When properly mounted, the elevation screw (marked "UP") should be on top and the windage screw (marked "L") on the left side with respect to the rifle. When position of mount rings is found to be correct, tighten the mount ring screws, after checking cross hairs.

(4) Check the cross hairs to see that they are exactly vertical and horizontal in the tube when mounted and, if necessary to correct alinement, adjust sight with respect to the mount base by loosening mount ring screws and turning the tube in the rings as prescribed in paragraph 56, above.

NOTE: To facilitate sliding of mount rings on the sight tube or turning tube in rings, expand rings slightly by inserting blade of small screwdriver or other similar instrument in slit in ring. Mount ring screws should not be fully tightened until sight is mounted and checked for position of cross hairs. Observe above caution.

c. **Removal of Mount Rings.** The mount rings may be removed from the sight tube by loosening mount ring screws and sliding rings from tube in same general manner as when assembling.

59. CARE, CLEANING, AND LUBRICATION.

a. Rifles should be cleaned and oiled not later than the evening of the day on which they are fired, preferably immediately after cessation of firing, and should be inspected, cleaned and oiled daily for 3 days following cessation of firing.

MAINTENANCE AND REPAIR

b. The first step in cleaning is to remove the groups from the rifle as described in paragraph 7. This is sufficient for cleaning in the field (FM 23-10), but for a thorough cleaning of the rifle by trained ordnance personnel, the groups should be disassembled, as described in section II, so that each piece can be cleaned and oiled.

c. **Care and Cleaning of Bore, Chamber, and Metal Parts.** The bore should be thoroughly cleaned with CLEANER, rifle bore. This cleaner is a combination solvent and preservative issued for use by troops for cleaning small arms. When CLEANER, rifle bore, is not available, the bore should be cleaned with soap and hot water solution, SODA ASH and water solution (1½ spoonfuls per pint of water), hot water alone, or in the absence of these, cold water. To avoid possible injury to the rifling at the muzzle, rifle bores will be cleaned from the chamber end, the bolt being removed for this purpose.

(1) To use CLEANER, rifle bore, insert a clean patch, cut, in the slot in the cleaning rod and saturate it with cleaner. Push patch back and forth through bore several times, taking care that all points of the bore are cleaned from muzzle to chamber. Be sure the patch goes all the way through the bore before the direction is reversed. This will prevent the patch and rod from becoming stuck in the bore. While the bore is wet, a clean brush, if available, should be run all the way through and all the way back three or four times to remove any hardened particles in the bore. Remove the brush and run several patches saturated with cleaner, entirely through the bore, removing them from the muzzle end; then wipe the cleaning rod dry and, using dry clean patches, thoroughly swab the bore until it is perfectly dry. Clean chamber thoroughly in same general manner, using a patch wrapped around a stick if necessary. To use soap and hot water solution, SODA ASH and water solution, or water alone, follow the same procedure. Care should be taken to avoid wetting the wooden stock or guard. Examine the bore and chamber carefully for cleanliness. If they are not free from all residue repeat the cleaning process.

(2) Oil bore and chamber thoroughly, using the cleaning rod and clean cut patches saturated with OIL, lubricating, preservative, special. The bore and chamber must be wiped completely dry of oil before firing the rifle.

(3) Use clean dry CLOTH, wiping, for cleaning all parts of the rifle other than the bore and chamber; then wipe the parts with clean CLOTH, wiping, dampened with oil and well wrung out. At all atmospheric temperatures OIL, lubricating, preservative, special, is suitable for this purpose. Excessive oiling is a waste of oil and results in a collection of dirt which causes friction and wear. In weather below freezing, care should be taken to use oil very sparingly, after careful cleaning of all parts. For care of weapons in extremely cold weather, refer to paragraph 61.

ORDNANCE MAINTENANCE — U.S. RIFLES, CAL. .30,
M1903, M1903A1, M1903A3 AND M1903A4

(4) In active service, use OIL, lubricating, preservative, special, for daily application or as a rust-preventive for short periods where daily inspection is possible. The weapon will be thoroughly cleaned and reoiled every 5 days. For surf landing operations or where high humidity or salt water spray is present, use OIL, lubricating, preservative, medium. To prepare the weapon for storage, refer to paragraph 64.

d. Care of the Rifle Stock. About once a month apply OIL, linseed, raw, with a CLOTH, wiping, to the wood. The surplus oil should be wiped off and the stock polished with a clean dry cloth or the palm of the hand. Care must be exercised not to allow the oil to get into the mechanism of the rifle as it will harden and prevent functioning. The stock and hand guard or barrel guard should be removed from the barrel and receiver for such oiling.

e. Care and Cleaning of Bayonet, Bayonet Scabbard, and Gun Sling.

(1) BAYONET. The bayonet should be cleaned and then wiped with slightly oiled CLOTH, wiping, care being taken not to use enough oil to allow transfer to the scabbard. Use OIL, lubricating, preservative, special.

(2) BAYONET SCABBARD. The bayonet scabbard may be washed on the outside with water and castile soap, rinsed with clean water, and dried. The mouth and hooks should then be wiped with slightly oiled CLOTH, wiping, care being taken not to get oil on the fabric cover (Scabbard M1910). Use OIL, lubricating, preservative, special.

(3) GUN SLING. The gun sling should be washed with water and castile or saddle soap, rinsed with clean water, and dried. When dry, OIL, neat's-foot, may be applied (if leather is hard), with CLOTH, wiping. Rub oil well into leather. Do not use an excessive amount of oil as it will take a long time to dry and may mark clothing. After oil is dry, the sling may be polished with DRESSING, russet leather. If leather is pliable and in good condition it may be treated with a thick lather of saddle soap, rinsed with clean water, and when thoroughly dry, rubbed briskly with clean, dry CLOTH, wiping.

60. CARE OF TELESCOPIC SIGHT.

a. Care, cleaning, and oiling of the telescopic sight used on the Rifle M1903A4 is explained in detail in TM 9-270.

Section V

SPECIAL MAINTENANCE

61. CARE OF MATERIEL IN BELOW FREEZING TEMPERA-TURES.

a. Special care, cleaning, and lubrication of the rifle is necessary for its proper functioning when low temperatures are encountered. In temperatures below freezing, it is necessary that the moving parts of the rifle be kept absolutely free of moisture. It has been found that excess oil on the working parts will solidify to such an extent as to cause sluggish operation or complete failure.

b. Upon being brought indoors, the rifle should first be allowed to come to room temperature. It should then be disassembled, wiped completely dry of the moisture which will have condensed on the cold metal surfaces, and thoroughly oiled with OIL, lubricating, preservative, special. Oiling is best done by wiping with a clean cloth, dampened with oil and *well wrung out*. If the rifle has been fired, it should be cleaned as described in paragraph 59.

c. If possible, condensation should be avoided by providing a cold place in which to keep rifles when not in use; for example, a separate cold room with appropriate racks may be used or, when in the field, racks under proper cover may be set up outdoors.

d. Before use, the metal parts of the rifle should be disassembled and completely cleaned with SOLVENT, dry-cleaning. The parts should then be completely dried with clean, dry, lintless CLOTH, wiping, and lightly oiled with OIL, lubricating, preservative, special, and again wiped dry. SOLVENT, dry-cleaning, removes every trace of oil and grease, hence metal is susceptible to quick rusting and should not be handled with bare hands until oiled. The working surfaces and parts which show signs of wear may be lightly lubricated by wiping with a cloth which has been saturated with OIL, lubricating, preservative, special, and then wrung out.

e. Care of the telescopic sight used on the Rifle M1903A4, is explained in TM 9-270.

f. The bayonets used with the rifles should be cared for in a similar manner, but may be kept lightly oiled at all times with OIL, lubricating, preservative, special. The metal parts of bayonet scabbards should be cared for in like manner.

62. CARE OF MATERIEL UNDER EXTREME HIGH TEMPERATURES.

a. Hot, Humid Areas.

(1) Where temperature and humidity are high, where salt air is present, or during rainy seasons, the weapon should be thoroughly inspected daily and kept lightly oiled when not in use. The groups should be dismounted at regular intervals and, if necessary, disassembled sufficiently to enable the drying and oiling of parts.

(2) Care should be exercised to see that unexposed parts and surfaces are kept clean and oiled, and rifles should be inspected frequently.

(3) OIL, lubricating, preservative, medium, should be used for oiling and lubrication.

(4) Wood parts should also be inspected to see that swelling due to moisture does not bind working parts. (In such cases shave off wood *only enough* to relieve binding.) A light coat of raw linseed oil applied at intervals and well rubbed in with the heel of the hand, will help to keep moisture out. Allow oil to soak in for a few hours and then wipe and polish wood with dry, clean CLOTH, wiping.

NOTE: Care should be taken that linseed oil does not get into the mechanism or on metal parts, as it will become gummy when dry. Stock and hand guard should be dismounted when this oil is applied.

b. Hot, Dry Areas.

(1) In hot, dry areas where sand and dust are apt to get into the mechanism and bore, the weapon should be wiped clean daily, or oftener, if necessary. Groups should be dismounted and disassembled as far as necessary to facilitate thorough cleaning.

(2) When the weapon is being used under sandy conditions, all lubricant should be wiped from the weapon. This will prevent sand carried by the wind from sticking to the lubricant and forming an abrasive compound which will ruin the mechanism. Immediately upon leaving sandy terrain, the weapon must be thoroughly cleaned and relubricated with OIL, lubricating, preservative, special.

(3) In such climates, wood parts are apt to dry out and shrink, and a *light* application of raw linseed oil applied as in subparagraph **a** (4), above, will help to keep wood in condition.

(4) Perspiration from the hands is a contributing factor to rust because it contains acid, and metal parts should be wiped dry frequently.

(5) During sand or dust storms, rifle should be kept covered, if possible, the breech and muzzle especially.

c. Care of the telescopic sight used on the Rifle M1903A4 is explained in TM 9-270.

d. The bayonets and bayonet scabbards used with the rifles should be cared for in a similar manner, and frequently inspected for rust.

SPECIAL MAINTENANCE

63. CLEANING MATERIEL RECEIVED FROM STORAGE.

a. Rifles which have been stored in accordance with paragraph 64, will be coated with either OIL, lubricating, preservative, light; OIL, lubricating, preservative, medium; or COMPOUND, rust-preventive, light or heavy. Completely disassemble rifle and use SOLVENT, dry-cleaning, to remove all traces of the compound or oil, particular care being taken that the bore, chamber, and all recesses in which springs or plungers operate are cleaned thoroughly. Completely remove SOLVENT, dry-cleaning, from all parts, using clean, CLOTH, wiping. Then oil and lubricate immediately as prescribed in paragraphs 59, 61, or 62, depending upon conditions.

CAUTION: Failure to clean the firing pin, spring, and striker and the tunnel in the bolt in which they operate, may result in gun failure at normal temperatures and will most certainly result in serious malfunctions if the rifles are operated in low temperature areas, as rust-preventive compound and excessive lubricating oil will congeal on the mechanism.

b. SOLVENT, dry-cleaning, is an inflammable, noncorrosive petroleum distillate, used for removing grease. *It should not be used near open flame and smoking is prohibited when it is being used.* It is generally applied by swabbing large parts and as a bath for small parts. The surfaces cleaned must be thoroughly dried to remove the solvent, and then *immediately* oiled to prevent rusting. To avoid leaving finger marks, which are ordinarily acid and induce corrosion, gloves should be worn by persons handling parts after such cleaning. SOLVENT, dry-cleaning, will attack and discolor rubber. In a emergency, oil, fuel, Diesel, may be used. Gasoline is dangerous and prohibited.

c. If SOLVENT, dry-cleaning, or OIL, fuel, Diesel, are not available, a solution of boiling water and issue soap, or SODA ASH may be used. SODA ASH should be used in the proportion of ½ pound to 1 gallon of warm water. The metal parts of the rifle and bayonet should be disassembled and placed in a wire basket and then completely immersed in the boiling solution for about ½ hour. Skim the rust-preventive compound off the top of the water to insure that particles of it will not adhere to the clean components when removed from the bath. Dry parts thoroughly with dry, clean, lintless CLOTH, wiping, wearing gloves during the process. Then oil immediately as prescribed in subparagraph a, above. Care should be used to prevent the solution from getting in eyes, or from prolonged contact with skin. It will attack galvanized and nonferrous metals. For detailed use of the above, refer to TM 9-850. Never use water and lye or any caustic to clean rifles, as it will attack the metal.

NOTE: As SOLVENT, dry-cleaning, or other degreasers completely remove all oil or grease, leaving cleaned surface entirely un-

ORDNANCE MAINTENANCE — U.S. RIFLES, CAL. .30,
M1903, M1903A1, M1903A3 AND M1903A4

protected, metal parts should be immediately oiled or greased, as prescribed herein, according to conditions, to prevent rusting.

d. Great care should be used when removing oil and grease from
the telescopic sight used on the Rifle M1903A4. Cleaning should be
done with clean, dry wiping cloths. The sight must not be dipped,
or SOLVENT, dry-cleaning, used, as liquid may penetrate the joints
of the tube or lenses. The exterior of the lenses may be cleaned carefully with ALCOHOL, ethyl or SOAP, liquid, lens cleaning, to remove
any oil, or grease, as explained in TM 9-270.

e. Bayonets may be disassembled and cleaned in a similar manner
to the rifle. Bayonet scabbards should not be dipped; the oil or
grease should be removed by wiping with a clean, dry, wiping cloth.

64. PREPARING MATERIEL FOR STORAGE.

a. OIL, Lubricating, Preservative, Medium. This oil is efficient
for preserving the polished surfaces, the bore, and the chamber of rifles
for periods up to 1 year, dependent on the climatic and storage conditions. Rifles in short-term storage should be inspected frequently
wherever possible and preservative film renewed if necessary. After
a copious application or after dipping the rifle in the oil at normal
temperature, wrap the rifle in greaseproof paper. This method can be
depended upon for the necessary protection particularly if regularly
scheduled inspection cannot be undertaken.

b. COMPOUND, Rust-preventive, Light. This compound is a
semisolid material. The compound is efficient for preserving the
polished metal surfaces, the bore, and the chamber for a period of
1 year or less, dependent on the climatic and storage conditions. It
is best applied by reducing compound to a fluid state by indirect
heating as explained in subparagraph c, below. The compound can
then be applied as described in subparagraph d, below. If heating
facilities are not available, the compound can be brushed on at
temperature as low as 60 F.

c. COMPOUND, Rust-preventive, Heavy. This compound is a
very viscous petroleum product, used for the protection of finished
metal surfaces during dead storage. It may be heated in a suitable
tank so that the parts of the rifle may be coated by dipping. It is
inflammable, and precautions must be taken to avoid overheating.
The compound must not be heated over an open flame. A practical
method for obtaining fluidity is to place container in a vessel of water,
heating it to a temperature of about 180 F, the exact temperature
being determined by the thickness of the film desired. The higher the
temperature of the grease, the thinner is the film applied to the metal.
The best temperature is that at which the grease is fluid enough to
form a uniform film of the maximum thickness which can be retained

SPECIAL MAINTENANCE

on the metal in storage. The grease should be heated to the temperature at which used for about half an hour before using. Best results will be obtained if the compound is heated slightly above this temperature and then allowed to cool to the desired consistency before using. During heating, the compound should be stirred to eliminate bubbles of air or water vapor. Presence of water will be indicated by frothing on the top of the bath. For detailed explanation of use and specifications of materials used, refer to TM 9-850 and SNL K-1, respectively.

d. The rifle should be cleaned and prepared with particular care. The bore, all parts of the mechanism, and the exterior of the rifle should be thoroughly cleaned with SOLVENT, dry-cleaning, and then dried completely with clean, dry CLOTH, wiping. In damp climates, particular care must be taken to see that the cloths are dry. After drying a metal part, the bare hands should not touch that part. All metal parts should then be immediately coated either with OIL, lubricating, preservative, medium, or COMPOUND, rust-preventive, light, or COMPOUND, rust-preventive, heavy, depending on the length of storage, the facilities available, and the frequency at which it is anticipated inspection will be made (subpars. a, b, and c, above). Aside from dipping the whole rifle, application of the protective film to the bore of the rifle is best done by dipping the cleaning brush in the preservative and running it through the bore two or three times. (Cleaning brush must be clean.) Before placing the rifle in the packing chest, see that the bolt is in its forward position and that the firing mechanism is released. Then handling the rifle by the wooden parts only, it should be placed in the packing chest, the wooden supports at the butt and muzzle having previously been painted with the preservative rust-preventive. Under no circumstances should a rifle contained in a cloth cover or with a plug in the bore, be placed in storage. Such articles collect moisture which causes the weapon to rust. To prevent the preservative with which the muzzle and butt are coated from being absorbed by the wooden supports of the chest, seal the muzzle and breech ends with two layers of PAPER, greaseproof, Kraft, wrapping, waterproofed, and secure with TAPE, adhesive, non-hygroscopic.

e. To prepare the bayonet for storage, remove it from the scabbard, disassemble, and clean thoroughly, and apply OIL, lubricating, preservative, medium, or rust-preventive compound to the metal parts, as for the rifle. Do not replace the bayonet in the scabbard. The bayonet should then be wrapped in greaseproof paper.

f. The bayonet scabbard should be thoroughly cleaned, but not allowed to come in contact with any oil or grease. The metal parts may be oiled lightly with OIL, lubricating, preservative, medium, and the scabbard then wrapped in greaseproof paper.

g. Great care must be used when preparing the telescopic sights

ORDNANCE MAINTENANCE — U.S. RIFLES, CAL. .30, M1903, M1903A1, M1903A3 AND M1903A4

used on the Rifle M1903A4 for storage. The mount rings should be removed and the sight thoroughly cleaned with clean, dry wiping cloths. A little OIL, lubricating, preservative, medium, may be applied to the cloth if necessary, but care must be taken that the oil does not get on the lenses. The lenses should be cleaned with ALCOHOL, ethyl, or SOAP, liquid, lens cleaning, as explained in TM 9-270, to remove any dirt, oil, or grease. The outside of the sight tube should then be *lightly* coated with OIL, lubricating, preservative, medium, observing great care that oil does not get on lenses. Such coating should be done with clean, CLOTH, wiping, lightly saturated with the oil used. The sight should then be wrapped in greaseproof and waterproof paper.

h. Leather gun slings should be thoroughly cleaned and then given a coat of OIL, neat's-foot, before storing.

65. PACKING MATERIEL FOR SHIPMENT OR STORAGE.

a. The packing of the rifle and its appendages and accessories, the bayonet and bayonet scabbard, for shipment or storage should be preceded by preparing the materiel as described in paragraph 64 of this manual.

b. The essential data necessary in the determination of storage space and shipping requirements for this materiel when packed in standard containers are given in SNL B-3 and OSSC B, "Ordnance Storage and Shipment Chart, Group B—Major Items."

c. Instructions for the marking of the outside of packages and items to be shipped to the Ordnance Department or other branches of the U. S. Army, whether from manufacturers or from depots or other military units, will be found in IOSSC-(b), "Introduction to Ordnance Storage and Shipment Charts, Section (b)—Instructions for Marking Shipments of Ordnance Supplies."

66. DEFENSE AGAINST CHEMICAL ATTACK, AND DECONTAMINATION OF MATERIEL.

a. For defense against chemical attack, refer to FM 21-40 listed in paragraph 69.

b. For method of decontaminating materiel subjected to chemical attack, and materials used, refer to TM 3-220, listed in paragraph 69.

Section VI
REFERENCES

67. PUBLICATIONS INDEXES.

The following publications indexes should be consulted frequently for latest changes or revisions of references given in this section and for new publications relating to materiel covered in this manual:

a. Introduction to Ordnance Catalog (explaining SNL system) .... ASF Cat. ORD 1 IOC

b. Ordnance Publications for Supply Index (index to SNL's) .... ASF Cat. ORD 2 OPSI

c. Index to Ordnance Publications (listing FM's, TM's, TC's, and TB's of interest to ordnance personnel, OPSR, MWO's, BSR, S or SR's, OSSC's, and OFSB's, and includes Alphabetical List of Major Items with Publications Pertaining Thereto) .... OFSB 1-1

d. List of Publications for Training (listing MR's, MTP's, T/BA's, T/A's, FM's, TM's, and TR's concerning training) .... FM 21-6

e. List of Training Films, Film Strips, and Film Bulletins (listing TF's, FS's, and FB's by serial number and subject) .... FM 21-7

f. Military Training Aids (listing Graphic Training Aids, Models, Devices, and Displays) ... FM 21-8

68. STANDARD NOMENCLATURE LISTS.

a. Cleaning and Preserving.
Cleaning, preserving and lubricating materials; recoil fluids; special oils, and miscellaneous related items .... SNL K-1
Soldering, brazing and welding material, gases and related items .... SNL K-2

b. Gun Materiel.
Ammunition, rifle, carbine, and automatic gun .. SNL T-1
Bayonets and their scabbards .... SNL B-8
Rifles, U. S., cal. .30, M1903, M1903A1, M1903A3, and M1903A4 (Snipers) ...... SNL B-3

c. Repair.
Tools, maintenance, for repair of, small and hand arms, and pyrotechnic projectors ..... SNL B-20

ORDNANCE MAINTENANCE — U.S. RIFLES, CAL. .30, M1903, M1903A1, M1903A3 AND M1903A4

Truck, 2½-ton, 6 x 6, small arms repair,
M7 and M7A1 . . . .   SNL G-138
Truck, small arms repair, M1 . . . .   SNL G-72

69. EXPLANATORY PUBLICATIONS.

a. **Chemical Attack and Decontamination.**
Chemical Decontamination Materials and
  equipment . . . .   TM 3-220
Defense against chemical attack . . . .   FM 21-40
Military chemistry and chemical agents . . . . . .   TM 3-215

b. **Gun Materiel.**
Ammunition, general . . . .   TM 9-1900
Small arms ammunition . . . .   TM 9-1990
U. S. rifle, cal. .30, M1903 . . . .   FM 23-10
U. S. rifle, cal. .30, M1903A4 (Snipers), charac-
  teristics and operation; and use of telescopic
  sight . . . .   TM 9-270

c. **Inspection, Maintenance, and Lubrication.**
Cleaning, preserving, lubricating, and welding
  materials and similar items issued by the
  Ordnance Department . . . .   TM 9-850
General lubrication instructions, small arms
  (31 May 1943) . . . .   OFSB 6-3
Inspection of ordnance materiel . . . .   TM 9-1100

d. **Storage and Shipment.**
Introduction to ordnance storage and shipment
  charts . . . .   IOSSC-(b)
Ordnance storage and shipment chart—group
  B—major items . . . .   OSSC B

INDEX

ORDNANCE MAINTENANCE — U.S. RIFLES, CAL. .30, M1903, M1903A1, M1903A3 AND M1903A4

INDEX

ORDNANCE MAINTENANCE — U.S. RIFLES, CAL. .30, M1903, M1903A1, M1903A3 AND M1903A4

PUBLICATIONS DEPARTMENT — RARITAN ARSENAL

www.ingramcontent.com/pod-product-compliance
Lightning Source LLC
LaVergne TN
LVHW021521080426
835509LV00018B/2592